Introduction

A 'Topic' is an approach to teaching in a Primary School which involves various apparently unrelated tasks being carried out under the umbrella of a common title or theme such as 'Ancient Egypt'.

Topic work always:

- includes class, group and individual work with some element of choice.
- involves practical activities.
- uses themes selected which are thought appropriate to the interests and stage of development of the children involved.
- involves first hand experiences such as a visit or visitors.
- involves some sort of investigation.
- involves information gathering skills.
- crosses some curriculum boundaries.

    It should also include, if possible, an element of *FUN*.

The purpose of this book is to provide a bank of ideas and photocopiable activities, based on the study of Ancient Egypt, which fulfil the above criteria. It is envisaged that a busy class teacher will use his or her professional judgement to select activities appropriate to their own individual situation.

Topical Resources publishes a range of Educational Materials for use in Primary Schools and Pre-School Nurseries and Playgroups.

For latest catalogue:

Tel: 01772 863158

Fax: 01772 866153

E.Mail: sales@topical-resources.co.uk

For free sample pages, visit our website on:

www.topical-resources.co.uk

Copyright © 2003 Paul Cross

Illustrated by John Hutchinson

Printed in Great Britain for 'Topical Resources', Publishers of Educational Materials, P.O. Box 329, Broughton, Preston. PR3 5LT by T. Snape & Company Ltd., Boltons Court, Preston.

Typeset by Artworks, 69 Worden Lane, Leyland, Lancashire. PR5 2BD Tel: 01772 431010

First Published Feb 2003
ISBN 1-872977-73-1

Notes for Teachers

Background Information for Class Lessons

Egypt Thrives Because of the River Nile

If you could have visited the thriving civilisation of Ancient Egypt at any time during its thirty centuries of history you would have found a place of marked contrasts. A narrow strip of land either side of the river Nile was fertile and green, made so by the waters of the Nile. The annual inundation caused by the melting of the snows and ice from the mountains of modern day Ethiopia meant that the soil on either bank of the Nile for about five miles was extremely fertile. Only in the delta region, where the Nile splits into slow flowing channels as it nears its journey's end in the Mediterranean sea, was this fertile strip widened beyond about ten miles. Beyond the delta and the Nile's fertile strip was the desert, a sun baked, arid area with little rain fall and a few scattered watering holes at oasis points. It was an inhospitable area subject to fierce skin scorching sand storms.

The Ancient Egyptians gave these two distinctively different areas names which originate from their soil colourings; so the desert was the Red Earth and the fertile Nile flood plain was called the Black Earth. The annual flooding brought rich soils to add to the already fertile earth. It meant that the farming people living close to the Nile migrated to higher ground for the flood months of September and October. The Ancient Egyptians did not understand the causes of the annual flooding but they knew that their prosperity came from the rich variety of animal and plant life that prospered on the rich soil. So in praise of this the Egyptians raised Hapi the God of the Nile to a high status. Thousands of copies of their song of praise to him survive showing his importance to their lives. The hymn's first line sums up the Nile's importance in the creation of the riches of the Ancient Egypt, " Hail to you O Nile , who issues from the earth and comes to keep Egypt alive."

Pre Historic Settlements in Egypt

The fertility of the soil attracted a large range of wild life species to the Nile Valley. This in turn was the reason why human beings were attracted to the area. Historians and archaeologists can provide us with no reliable date or place of origin for the migration of humans into the Nile region. Hunter gatherers would be attracted from the areas around Egypt where the desert was expanding and ruining their hunting grounds. Sometime around 6000 B.C. people settled in the Nile valley and began to plant crops such as wheat and barley, and to raise domesticated animals such as cattle, sheep and goats. They settled into villages and built mud brick dwellings. Their stone tools have been found as have pieces of their domestic pottery. Pottery and stone figures show they developed their own forms of religion. Archaeologists are able to tell us that over hundreds and thousands of years these prehistoric settlements became larger, that small kingdoms with their own kings developed, and that these kingdoms became united into two major kingdoms. The Kingdom around the Delta of the Nile becoming known as the Kingdom of Lower Egypt. The land south of the delta, to the cataracts at Aswan, became known as the Kingdom of Upper Egypt.

The Kingdoms and Dynasties of Ancient Egypt

The first factor to grasp firmly in any study of this historical period is that the civilisations that we unite under the title of 'Ancient Egypt' lasted for three thousand years, longer than any other civilisation in history. Historians have divided the thirty centuries long Ancient Egyptian period into Dynasties and Kingdoms. These divisions are based on the writings of Manetho, an Egyptian priest from 250 B.C. as well as evidence from many other archaeological sources. It is interesting to note that the dating of these periods of the Ancient Egyptian civilisations start at the same era as the first simple form of writing in hieroglyphics commences. For a study at Key Stage 2 level it is not necessary to know all the dynasties and periods. An outline of the more salient parts of the period are all that is necessary.

The Archaic Period (3200 to 2680 B.C.)

King Menes ruler of upper Egypt was powerful enough to conquer all the small kingdoms that made up Lower Egypt. He built a new capital city at Memphis. He had great wealth which is shown by the quality and variety of goods found in his and his successors' rectangular tombs at Abydos and Saqquara. It is from this period that the earliest simple hieroglyphics date.

The Old Kingdom (2680 to 2180 B.C.)

This was the first period of great wealth for Egypt, shown in the building of the Step Pyramid at Saqquara by King Zoser circa 2630 B.C., and the Great Pyramid at Giza built by Khufu around 2538 B.C. and his successors' pyramids at Giza. The jewellery, household goods and other richly decorated tomb objects show Ancient Egypt's growing trade with Nubia to the south west, Lebanon to the north east, and Punt to the south east. The building of these huge tomb monuments illustrates the highly organised and centralised nature of Egyptian society in this period. Clearly a Pharaoh, who could organise and have carried out such an expensive building project merely for his tomb, had a hugely powerful position. No wonder that Temple carvings of the Pharaohs and their consorts of this period

Background Information for Class Lessons

show them on a par with the gods of Ancient Egypt.

Invaders Take Over Egypt (1630 to 1560 B.C.)

After one thousand years of strong centralised government by various family dynasties, interspersed by periods of civil war between ruling families, or within the families of Pharaohs, Egypt suffered a period of invasion and occupation. Taking advantage of a period of internal weakness and quarrelling, a people known as the Hyksos, from the region of the Red Sea, invaded and conquered Lower Egypt. They speedily formed an alliance with the Nubians to the south west of Egypt to control the whole of Egypt. Whilst the Hyksos people soon assimilated Egyptian ways completely, their very presence was deeply resented by Egyptians. Struggles within Egypt kept breaking out as native Egyptians sought ways in which the foriegners could be expelled. The family of the Prince of Thebes organised a growing resistance to the Hyksos rulers, which eventually led to their total expulsion from Egypt by 1560 B.C.

The New Kingdom (1560 to 1085 B.C.)

A strong feeling of national pride, which naturally followed the victory over the Hyksos tribe, was coupled with the technological development of the horse drawn chariot. This mobile fighting machine led to a period of expansion and the creation of an Egyptian Empire. A succession of fierce warrior Pharaohs conquered an area from the Euphrates in the north east to the southern most border of the former kingdom of Nubia.

Loot from these invasions was followed by annual tribute owed to the Egyptian Pharaohs by the conquered peoples. Trade was then centred on Egypt and a period of extreme wealth followed for the ruling elite of the country. This huge wealth was manifested in even richer tomb articles and elaborately decorated temples, many dedicated to the King of Ancient Egyptian Gods Amun, who was thought to have brought Egypt her recent victories.

The strengthened worship of Amun meant that the priests serving him, became more and more powerful in Egyptian society.

As if in response to this growing power, the next Pharaoh Akenaten left the traditional capital of Egypt, Thebes. He made himself a new capital and a richly decorated Temple to his new god of the disc of the sun, Aten. However, this radical change in the centuries of Egyptian worship was resisted and Akenaten was murdered in mysterious circumstances.

His successor Tutenkhamun restored the capital to Thebes and might have gone on to a more glorious future but for his early death. For us now the young Pharaoh is more famous because of Howard Carter's discovery of the fabulous treasures with which he was surrounded for his journey into the after life. The mask from Tutenkhamun's sarcophagus surely is the most famous of all artefacts from the whole of history.

A series of weak Pharaohs following Tutenkhamun meant that a new tribe of Israelites, the Hittites, conquered most of the former Egyptian Empire. Egypt itself grew ever weaker as priests and officials ruled the land acting on behalf of young and weak Pharaohs. Egypt was threatened by raids by Nubians, Philistines and the Hittites.

The emergence of a powerful warrior Pharaoh, Rameses III, thrust back Egypt's enemies. However, the respite was only temporary as the period from 1085 to 332 B.C. was filled with invasions of the land of the Pharaohs. Assyrians, Philistines then Persians, attacked and conquered Egypt. This unsettled and lawless period was the time when so many of the treasures of the Tombs of Ancient Egypt were raided by tomb robbers.

The Ptolemaic Period (332 to 30 B.C.)

The brilliant warrior king of Greece Alexander the Great invaded Egypt in his campaign against the Persians. His victory ensured the departure of the hated Persians from Egyptian soil. This endeared him and his army to the native Egyptians, so much so that one of his generals Ptolemy, left in charge of Egypt after Alexander's departure for campaigns in Asia, was created Pharaoh. Ptolemy's family ruled Egypt for the next three hundred years, bringing many facets of Greek culture to blend with those of Ancient Egypt. The last Ptolemaic Pharaoh Cleopatra, infatuated by her Roman visitor Mark Anthony, allied Egypt to his side in the Roman civil war. Octavius Caesar, summoning loyal Roman forces, invaded Egypt, defeated and killed Mark Anthony. His total victory was denied by Cleopatra's famous suicide. Egypt became a Roman province. The next time it was ruled by an Egyptian was as recently as 1956 A.D.

The Structure of Egyptian Society

Egyptian society can be compared to one face of a pyramid. At the tip are the Pharaohs and their immediate family. They are at the summit of society, when all is well with the Pharaoh, all is well with Egypt. From his family, when all is well, you would expect the next Pharaoh to come. Throughout the long period known as Ancient Egypt many different families held power as Pharaohs. The Pharaoh ordered society, if his orders were good then Egypt flourished. If the Pharaoh failed with his orders then…

Background Information for Class Lessons

Next layer down, the pyramid's side widens slightly. Here in Ancient Egyptian society were the courtiers, high priests, and high officials and members of the ruling class who owned large areas of land. Society expected them to ensure by their orders and organisation that the Pharaoh's wishes were carried out. They needed to be strong if Egypt was to prosper. In times of an ineffective Pharaoh it was from this level of society that an alternative future Pharaoh came.

Next came the middle layer of the pyramid, large and well spread in number. Here were found the educated classes, the scribes, the local and national government officials, the priests and priestesses, doctors, engineers, architects and soldiers. They had a two way role. First they supplied the facts, on which decisions higher up society were made. They were also the vital building blocks that ensured that the Pharaoh's decisions were carried out locally and recorded for posterity as well as for the Pharaoh.

The next layer of the pyramid, and Ancient Egyptian society, was wide, taking in a large section of the populace. Here, were those with skills and specialities which were valued by Egyptian society. Craftsmen and women, entertainers, and the palace's and higher official's servants formed this hard working yet highly skilled people. The treasures of Ancient Egypt that we marvel at were their creation. At the base of Ancient Egyptian society were the peasant farmers, the labourers and the slaves. They supplied the muscles that fed and supplied Ancient Egypt's daily wants. They provided the muscle power for any project in the state. All these layers of society in Ancient Egypt could move place in the society. Slaves could become free, craftsmen, high officials could fail and be cast out or succeed and become Pharaohs. But every layer knew its place, its own importance, within Ancient Egyptian society.

The Gods and Goddesses of Ancient Egypt

The Ancient Egyptians worshipped hundreds of different gods and goddesses. Some had their own temples, some only had house shrines devoted to them, some were local to some small settlement. Some gods were represented by different symbols or animals in different places. Thus a baboon may be the sign for Thoth the god of wisdom in one place, whilst elsewhere a baboon stood for the moon god Khonsu.

It can however be safely stated that the main gods of Egypt were linked with the sun. At sunrise the sun god was Khepri, the scarab beetle rolling the sun across the sky. At midday the sun god was the hawk Re-Harakhty, soaring high above the earth. Later the sun god became Amun Re, responsible for all fertility, all creation, the god and protector of all creation.

Amongst other gods worth singling out for discussion in class lessons are Anubis, Horus, Hopi, Bastet and Seth. The god Anubis is represented with a jackal head as jackals were known to hang around cemeteries hoping for a meal. The jackal Anubis was the god of the dead and funerals, attendant at the embalming of mummies. Horus was hawk god, charged with keeping a watch over Egypt. He was the god of the Pharaohs as they watched over Egypt. Many Pharaohs claimed they were gods because of the importance of their work for Egypt. The god Hopi was equally important to Egyptians as he was the god of the Nile's inundation which annually brought a renewal of life to the Nile valley. Bastet was a cat shaped daughter of Amun Re the sun god, she was in charge of bringing the sun at harvest to ripen the crops. Her shrines in temples were surrounded by dead cats, sacrificed in the hope she would bring a bumper harvest to the people of Egypt. The hippopotamus shaped god Seth, was an embodiment of evil and violence, just like the wild hippos disturbed from their wallowing in the Nile mud. He would be called on to wreak havoc on your enemies whoever they might be.

The Ancient Egyptian Belief in the Afterlife

The Ancient Egyptians believed that below the earth there existed an underworld of lakes of fire, poisonous snakes and executioners which they called Duat. These hazards had to be passed through by dead people to reach the Hall of the Two Truths, where the dead person's heart was weighed against their past deeds. The ornate Books of the Dead, which have survived alongside most Ancient Egyptian mummies, were spells to help the dead person gain the afterlife through the dangers and tests of the Hall of Two Truths. Once the afterlife was achieved, breath would be breathed back into the mummified body and a new life would start. It was this chance of an other life that led to the practice of filling the tombs of rich Ancient Egyptians with goods, food and drink, that the person was thought to need in his or her new life. Statues of the dead as a young person were always found in these burial tombs, so that, should the body of the dead person be damaged in its journey through Duat, then life would be breathed into the statue and the dead person would start their afterlife as a young person again. As we know most about the Ancient Egyptians from these funereal goods, it was their belief and practices in the afterlife that has provided most evidence for archaeologists to inform us about life in Ancient Egypt.

Background Information for Class Lessons

Hieroglyphics, Hieratic Script and Demotic Scripts

Carvings, inscriptions and writing on papyrus paper survive from around 3100 B.C. These pieces of writing are really a series of pictures each one standing for different words or symbols, even letters. Archaeologists have collected over 1,000 different characters from this period of hierogylphic writing. It appears that the hierogylphic writing was kept complex so that only a long education and practice would enable the person to become fluent. In this way the secrets of the Pharaohs and their family and court could only be read about by society's elite. Scholars of Ancient Egyptian society surmise that only one person in a thousand in that society could read these early scripts.

From about 1780 B.C. the pictures that formed hieroglyphics are changed into an early form of symbols, the precursors of writing. These symbols are called hieratic writing. This development made for speedier recording and meant that exceptionally detailed records survive to inform us of the minutae of Ancient Egyptian everyday life. From around 600 B.C. an even more advanced form of writing developed called Demotic script came into use. By around 400 A.D. the understanding of the older forms of writing was lost, meaning that the inscriptions in the palaces and temples of Ancient Egypt were lost for centuries.

It was only when a stone with hieroglyphics, demotic and Greek scripts was found in 1799 at el- Rashid (or Rosetta) that work could start in unravelling the Hieroglyphic script. Finally in 1822 a Frenchman, Champollion, broke the code of all three forms of writing and unlocked the treasures of the riches of Ancient Egypt to scholars. From then onwards the meanings of papyrus documents, temple inscriptions and early stone carvings could be translated and our knowledge of the civilisation of Ancient Egypt reached a totally different level of understanding.

Buildings and Artefacts Reveal a High Level of Science, Technology and Mathematics

The earliest pyramid reveals a superb understanding of the science of astronomy, its sides face exactly the four points of the compass. Deep within the mass of the Great Pyramid at Giza lies the King's tomb room. Archaeologists have found that a narrow shaft was built piercing through the vast mass of stone work of the pyramid. This is an amazing feat of technological building work merely to align this shaft arrow-straight through the huge monolith of the pyramid. But that is dwarfed by the knowledge of the sun's relationship to the earth displayed by the Ancient designers and architects of the pyramid for at the summer solstice, the eyes of the Pharaoh Khufu's Mask in his sarcophagus, align through the shaft with the centre of the sun.

Further technological wonders in the building include the system of perfectly inclined slopes which aided the builders to move huge pieces of rock into position high up on the pyramid using highly trained and co-ordinated teams of men.

Papyrus documents dating from 850 B.C. reveal the Egyptians using a decimal system of number with separate symbols for ten, hundred and one thousand, to work out how much grain can be stored in a barn of a certain size. Cubit measures of 52centimetres survive with the length sub-divided into smaller units of palms and finger lengths. In a crowded land on the black soil of the Nile's banks the measurement of one's land was vital. More scrolls reveal that the Egyptians had worked out a calendar based on the sun's movements and using stone markers they could survive the Niles annual inundation, a good flood raised the level of the Nile by 7 metres, any more and damage would be widespread any less and a poor harvest would follow.

The craftsmanship shown in the fabulous artefacts from the tombs of the Pharaohs show a command of casting in precious metals, of cutting and setting precious stones in these metals, and making fine coloured glass.The superbly fine cloth of the rich Ancient Egyptians shows a mastery of the technology of spinning, weaving, printing and dyeing rare in the ancient world. The processes of mummification reveal a strong scientific study of the organs of the body, as well as a wide knowledge of chemicals present in rocks, herbs and roots that had preservative properties. The fact that those unique artefacts of Ancient Egypt, the mummified bodies of many of its people, have survived so long speaks volumes about the scientific skills of the Ancient Egyptians.

Buildings

Temple of the goddess Hathor at Dendera

Research into the surviving examples of Pyramid, Temple and Palace architecture of the Ancient Egyptian period will reveal lots of links to shape, symmetry and three dimensional mathematics. Concentrate on the rectangles, squares and triangles that form the basis of the construction of these marvellous buildings from five thousand to three thousand years ago. The children's three dimensional drawings will provide excellent practice in perspective and technical drawing.

More advanced observational three dimensional drawing can be given practice when the children study the opening up of Pyramids, Temples and Palaces to reveal exterior and interior three dimensional work. Reference books contain many of these examples for the children to use as models for their drawing.

Children's drawings collected together will make a fine architectural landscape for a classroom wall display.

Bas Relief Wall Sculptures and Murals

The children will enjoy the great variety of figure drawing and painting that the wall paintings and bas relief sculpture of the temples and palaces of Ancient Egypt present in the many reference sources of the period.

Give individuals, or groups of children mural design and painting tasks differentiated by subjects. For example some children will concentrate on dancing and music wall paintings, others on hunting subjects, others on animals. In this way the class may be able to cover the walls of the classroom with their murals.

Bas Relief work can be carried out by setting plaster in the top of a shoe box, allowing it to set well, then transferring a design to the plaster. Cut out the surrounding plaster with a pottery shaping tool then carefully paint the figure in relief. A selection of these will make a fine craft display.

Borders and Friezes

Many Ancient Egyptian pottery, mosaics and frescoes have decorated borders. Encourage the children to research in text books, CD ROMs and the internet to find examples of these borders and friezes.

The children's research should reveal foliage such as Papyrus and Lotus flowers, animals and human figures used repetitively as well as geometric patterns for friezes and borders. Use the children's patterns repeated in symmetrical form to edge their own work or for friezes around class work on Ancient Egypt. Encourage the children to use the bright oranges, reds, greens and blues so that their work will mirror that of Ancient Egyptian craftsmen.

Sculpture

The Ancient Egyptians were wonderful craftsmen in stone. Their work has come down to the present day to provide lots of ideas for the children's clay or plasticine modelling.

Take a subject such as the Gods of Ancient Egypt and reference books will provide sufficient painted stone models of the animal headed gods for each child in the class to produce their own individual god. Other subjects such as the Pharaohs and their wives, or the animals of Ancient Egypt could be sculpted in clay or plasticine and provide, when painted, a superb 3D display.

Rameses II at the Temple of Abu Simbel

Pharaoh's Jewelled Collar

Get the children to cut out two semi-circles of thick card, paint them lapis blue, and punch 3 holes along the straight edge.

Paint hollow pasta shapes in oranges, blues, turquoise and gold. When dry thread them along coloured thread. Attach three of these strings to the semicircular cards and you will have a class of Pharaohs wearing jewelled collars.

Use the same idea to make wrist bands for the children to wear on an Egyptian day.

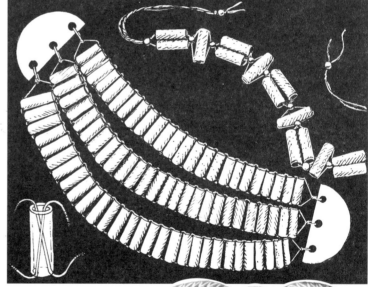

Jewelled collar and necklace

Amulets and Charms

Rich Ancient Egyptians were buried with amulets and charms which were to ward off evil and guide them on their passage to the After Life.

Make a 'Wedjet' or 'Eye of Horus' out of thick card and paint it orange, blue, red and black. This stylised eye was reputed to have healing powers. A similarly painted sacred Scarab (dung beetle) which was thought to stand for intelligence in the afterlife could be hung or placed on a class display of mummies.

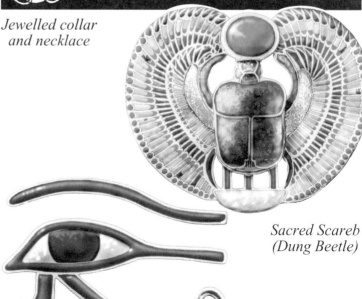

Sacred Scareb (Dung Beetle)

Wedjet

Art Ideas on the Theme of Ancient Egypt

Canopic Jars

These jars held the preserved internal organs of rich Egyptians. They were placed in their tomb with their former owner's mummified body.

They had the heads of a hawk, an ape, a jackal, and a human. Make them by adding paper mache pulp with lots of PVA glue to the lids of jars or plastic pots. Shape them into the required head adding more pulp and modelling it into the correct shape.

When dry paint them and later varnish with clear varnish.

Soak off any modern label from the glass jar and replace with an Ancient Egyptian Hieroglyphics sign.

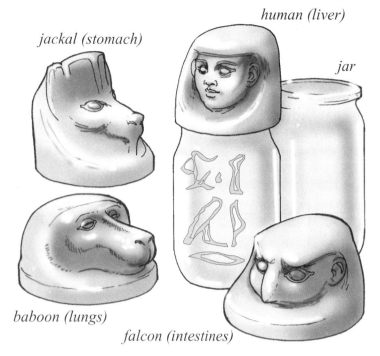

jackal (stomach)

human (liver)

jar

baboon (lungs)

falcon (intestines)

Egyptian Boxes

Ancient Egyptian tombs have preserved many boxes, brightly painted, holding the treasured articles of a dead person, ready for use again in the afterlife.

From rectangular, square and pyramid nets make cardboard boxes. Before pasting the net into its 3D shape, decorate all the surfaces with pictures of Ancient Egyptian gods, Pharaohs, hieroglyphics and borders.

The completed boxes would make excellent gift boxes for special events, but make sure the greetings label is in hieroglyphics.

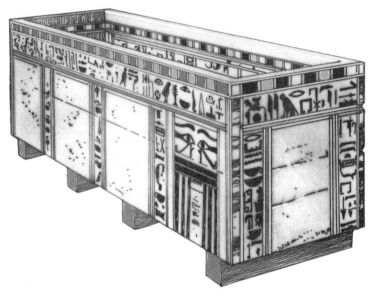

Good and Bad Beasts as Gods

The Ancient Egyptians chose their gods from the animals around their land. Seth an evil god was given the body of an angry male hippopotamus. Bastet, the cat shaped god, was a kindly and much loved god for children.

The hippo can have the body of a large pebble covered with paper strips and painted. Cut up cylinders for legs and a papier mache head can be glued on and painted bright blue.

Bastet can be made from a papier mache ball for a head stuck by lots of paper strips to the top of a cardboard cylinder. Decorate the body by crossing over blue and purple ribbons around the tube.

These 3D gods will form a very different temple display for a school entrance hall.

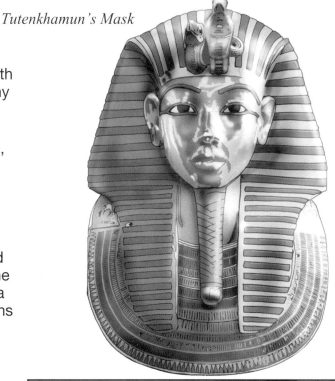

Tutenkhamun's Mask

Masks Leading to Costumes

Death masks over the faces of mummies are such a feature of Ancient Egyptian death that they should have pride of place in any Ancient Egyptian art display.

Papier mache over a blown up balloon, a clay shape, or modern modelling plastics, moulded into shape then painted in true Tutenkhamun style and varnished, will provide excellent costume extras for an Ancient Egyptian day.

Black paper strip wigs with hair bands, painted eyelids, Pharaoh's necklaces and white sheets run up as doublets, make the class ready for that Egyptian feast of pitta bread, olives, grapes, dates, kebabs, beans and goats cheese.

Scarab Seals

A personal clay seal, shaped as the dung beetle or scarab, applied with moist mud, would have secured your house or your tomb. Get the children to carefully model a mould in the shape of a scarab.

Fill the supported mould with plaster, allow to properly dry, then carve the rounded top into the features of the beetle.

Carve the underside with your own personal name in Hieroglyphics, or with your favourite Ancient Egyptian animal. Paint, and then you can stamp your seal on your possessions.

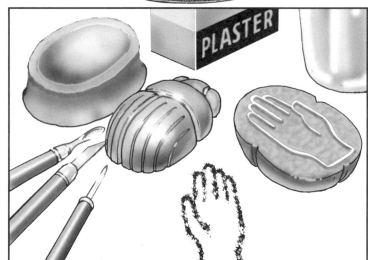

Picture Writing – Hieroglyphics

Change the whole of a class room wall into a wall in an Ancient Egyptian tomb, by giving each child a large rectangle of card, ask them to research for their twenty favourite picture writings or symbols, then get them to copy these large onto their rectangle. Paint these in bright oranges, purple, blue and gold on different background colours.

Then appoint guides to your class tomb, who will, of course, need their own self written information sheet to take other children on their 'Ancient Egyptian tomb tour'.

An Ancient Egyptian Timeline

Task A

Cut out each scarab beetle and paste it near to the correct place on the timeline of Ancient Egypt on the next two pages.

Some of the beetles do not have dates. You will have to research their dates from reference books.

Task B

Add further dates and facts to your timeline as you study Ancient Egypt.

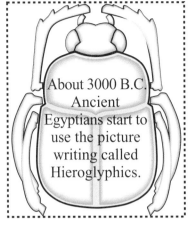
About 3000 B.C. Ancient Egyptians start to use the picture writing called Hieroglyphics.

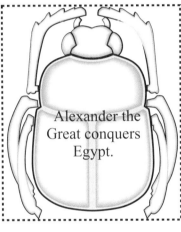
Alexander the Great conquers Egypt.

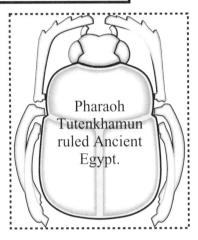
Pharaoh Tutenkhamun ruled Ancient Egypt.

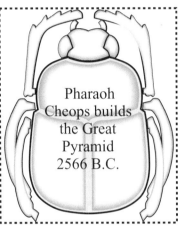
Pharaoh Cheops builds the Great Pyramid 2566 B.C.

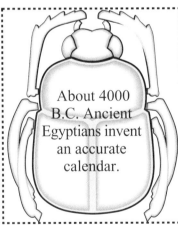
About 4000 B.C. Ancient Egyptians invent an accurate calendar.

Pharaoh Menes unites the two separate kingdoms of Lower and Upper Egypt 3100 B.C.

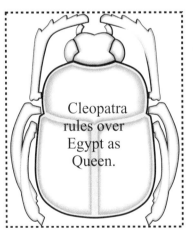
Cleopatra rules over Egypt as Queen.

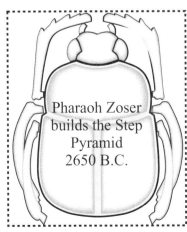
Pharaoh Zoser builds the Step Pyramid 2650 B.C.

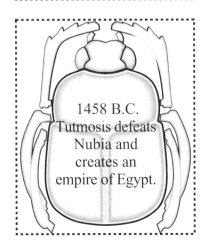
1458 B.C. Tutmosis defeats Nubia and creates an empire of Egypt.

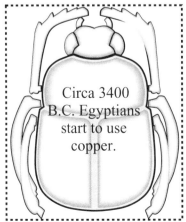
Circa 3400 B.C. Egyptians start to use copper.

An Ancient

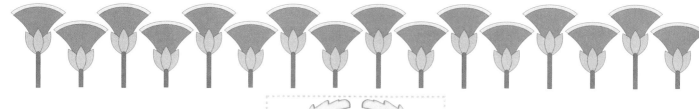

About 3000 B.C.
Ancient
Egyptians start to
use the picture
writing called
Hieroglyphics.

example

4000 BC	3900	3800	3700	3600	3500 BC	3400	3300	3200	3100	3000 BC	2900	2800	2700	2600	2500 BC	2400	2300	2200	2100	2000 BC

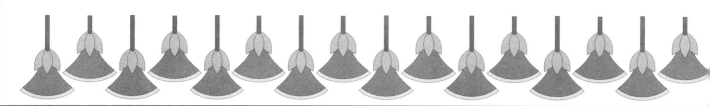

Egyptian Timeline

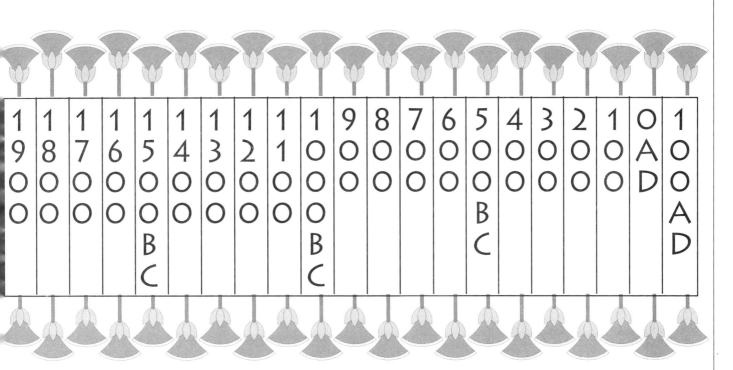

1900	1800	1700	1600	1500 BC	1400	1300	1200	1100	1000 BC	900	800	700	600	500 BC	400	300	200	100	0 AD	100 AD

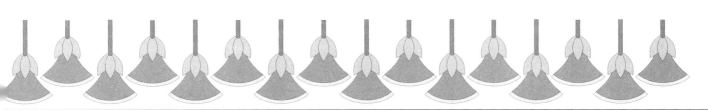

Different opinions about the building of the Sphinx

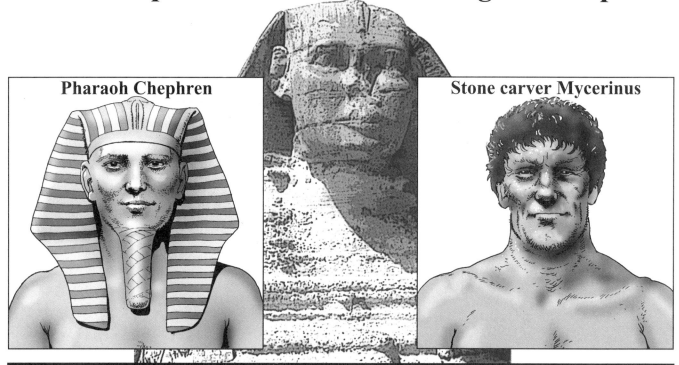

Pharaoh Chephren

Stone carver Mycerinus

Task A: Different Views of the Same Event

Cut out the Pharaoh and stone carver pictures above and paste them onto a separate piece of A4 paper.

Carefully read the statements below. Think about who might have made these comments, either Pharaoh Chephren or stone carver Mycerinus. Cut out each statement and paste it under the correct character on your own sheet.

The Sphinx shall have the body of a lion and a face like my own face.

I was ordered from my village to Giza. I had to take my working tools with me.

The stone was very easy to cut, it was softer than any I had worked on before.

My master craftsmen told me it would take three years to complete the carving of my Sphinx.

I will be buried in the Great Pyramid that is next to my Sphinx statue.

I work just after dawn as it is not so hot then. I have a rest in the shade in the middle of the day.

I hope to go back to my village to help with the harvest of the grain.

I had to stand very still whilst the master craftsman drew my face, for the Sphinx.

Yesterday the Great Pharaoh came to watch us at work.

I hope that my statue will soon be completed as I am getting older.

Task B.

Imagine you are a tomb robber coming at dead of night towards the Pyramid. Write down your feelings as the Sphinx gazes down on you in the moonlight. Next, pretend you are a guard as tomb robbers slink past the Sphinx towards you. Write what might happen next.

A Scribe's Equipment

Every part of Egyptian life was controlled by the Pharaohs, so they needed a very large band of Scribes to record all the orders for them. Scribes would spend a long time learning the Hieroglyphic writing, and practising their writing on pieces of broken pottery or stone before they were allowed to write on the expensive papyrus paper.

Hyrogliphic for scribe.

Can you see his water pot and palette?

Basic Clothes

A lot of the Scribes work was outside. He would wear a black wig on top of his shaven head. On top of this the Scribe would wear a round black woollen skull cap to protect him from the heat of the Sun. Scribes would wear a piece of white linen like a skirt tied at the waist. All scribes carried a stick to show their importance.

Papyrus Paper

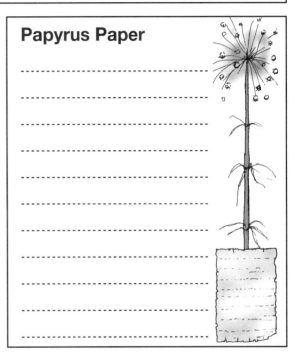

Hieroglyphics

Brushes

Rope

Twigs

Ruler & Palette

Ancient Egypian Transport

Artefacts

Archaeologists have dug up thousands of Ancient Egyptian objects including models, carvings, or paintings, showing us how people and goods were transported in the past.

On the staff of a fan from Tutenkhamun's tomb, are engravings of the king hunting wild animals. The Ancient Egyptians had copied the idea of the wheel from the Sumerian people. This also tells us that the Egyptians had trained horses to pull wheeled chariots.

A model in Tutenkhamun's tomb shows him using a small boat made from reeds to hunt in the marshes close to the River Nile. Many wall paintings show larger reed boats with sails being used to carry goods up and down the River Nile. Wood was scarce in Ancient Egypt so reed boats saved wood.

A stone carving shows a Pharaoh being carried in a chair on two poles on the shoulders of four slaves. These 'litters' would only be used for short journeys in the cities.

Stone carvings in the Temple at Thebes show slaves carrying large loads on their backs using a pole, with heavier loads carried on two poles between two men.

Written Evidence

Papyrus rolls with hieroglyphic writings tell us about food crops being brought to the Pharaoh's stores in reed baskets carried on donkeys.

A wooden model from a tomb in the Valley of the Kings shows us that wooden boats with sails, oars and large rudders were used for the heaviest of loads on the River Nile.

Task – Using Different Source Materials

Study each artefact, or piece of writing carefully. Write down what you have discovered about how the Ancient Egyptians moved about, or transported things on land and water.

Information from Artefacts

Wine Jar

Cooking Jar

Reed Baskets

Clay Oven

Bread

Rolling Dough

Wooden Roasting Spit

Oil Lamp

Pottery Storage Jar

Stone Mortar

Reed Fan

Metal Knife

Wooden spoon

Metal Cooking Grill

Wooden Chopping Board

Everyday Life in an Egyptian Noble's Villa

The Villa

Rich people lived in the countryside. Their homes were surrounded by walled gardens. They had separate rooms for men and women, a tiled bathroom, and a shrine room, where they would pray to their favourite god. They had many servants to care for their needs. The brick walls of the villa were decorated with fine wall paintings.

Keeping Cool

Thick walls with small windows set high in the walls kept many rooms cool. An outdoor pool surrounded by shady trees would be used in the heat of midday. The people living in the villa would keep cool by having cool water poured over them in the bathroom.

Furniture

Chairs, stools, beds, couches and storage chests would be made of wood with rich decoration added to them. Paint, carvings, gold and jewels decorated the objects. Fine paintings plus decorated wall and floor tiles would complete the rich rooms.

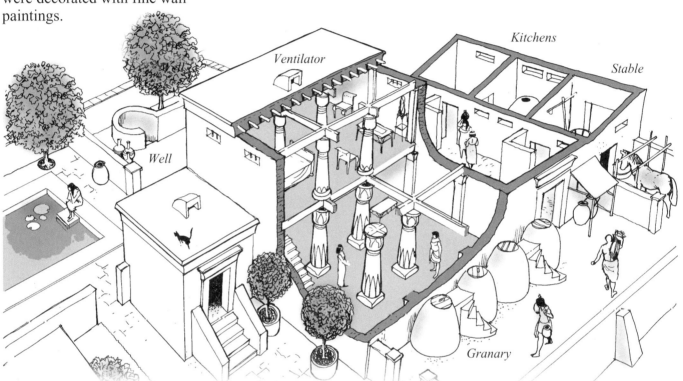

Keeping Clean

A separate bathroom with tiled walls and floors would be where the family members washed several times each day. Water was supplied from the villa's own well. In many rooms there would be a toilet stool with a pot inside it. Servants would empty the contents outside the villa's walls.

Food and Cooking

The many huge meals the noble's family would eat in the central hall would be prepared in the separate kitchen in the grounds of the villa.

Clay ovens and charcoal fired grills would be used to cook the food. The food would be stored in separate grain stores and huge jars in special stores.

Leisure Rooms

The women had separate rooms to relax in. There were also many separate bedrooms with fine beds. A separate large room would be used as the family's own 'temple', containing many statues and wall paintings of the Egyptian gods. There would be a scribe's room where the scribe worked for the noble and taught the children of the family.

Task – A Reasoning Exercise

1. After careful study of pages 18 and 19, choose which home you would have preferred to have lived in during Ancient Egyptian times. Give several reasons for your choice. Write your answers in full sentences.

2. Study pages 18 and 19 again. List 5 things that are different, and 5 things that are the same today. Write your answers in full sentences.

Everyday Life in an Egyptian Farmer's House

The House

Egyptian houses were built of mud bricks painted with white wash. The only wooden parts were the beams to hold the roof. The windows were high in the walls so that the sun did not make the rooms too hot.

Storing Food

Grain for making bread, dates, figs, raisins, pomegranates, onions, leek and garlic were stored in large pottery jars in the underground cellar to keep the food as cool as possible.

Beer made from old bread and water would be stored in large storage jars.

Cooking and Light

Bread was baked in clay ovens usually outside the house. Other cooking was done over charcoal fires outside to avoid the risk of fire in the house and to keep the house cool. Fans were used to create a very hot flame for cooking. Light at night was provided by small oil lamps.

Keeping Cool

In the hottest weather the family would spend most of their time on the roof, where the breeze would make life cooler.

An open roofed area made of River Nile rushes would make a cooler place to rest.

Furniture

The only furniture would be a wooden chest, and some rush baskets to store clothes and precious goods. There would also be a few wooden stools, a wooden table, and rush mats on the floor to sleep on.

Keeping Clean

A special stool with a hole in its centre was placed over a pot. This was the toilet. The contents were put on the land. People living in the house would wash either in the River Nile or in nearby drainage canals.

Task - Compare a rich villa with a farmer's home

Study the text and illustrations on pages 18 and 19. Complete your own copy of the chart below in as much detail as you can.

Topic	A Rich Egyptian's House	A Poor Egyptian's house
Keeping Cool		
Cooking		
Furniture		
Keeping Clean		

Using the Internet

How to find out more about Pharaoh Ramesses II's conquest of Nubia, Africa using the Internet, and how to print pictures of the event.

Check that the **Internet** page with the Address Box is on your screen.

1 Delete any address that is in the address box.

2 Type in *www.ancientegypt.co.uk*

3 Now either click on the address box or press the return key.

4 A picture of a lotus flower will open on your screen. Move your cursor over the word **Pharaoh** at the left hand side of the screen and click with your mouse.

5 A page concerning the Pharaoh's as Lords of both parts of Egypt will appear. When you have read the page click on the word **story** at the left hand side of the screen with your mouse.

6 You will now have 13 pages of an illustrated story about Rameses' II battle in Nubia and how the the Egyptians won the battle. Study the text and pictures carefully, then select which picture you would like to print out.

7 Make sure your printer is switched on, then **highlight** the picture, with some text that accompanies it, by dragging the cursor over it **holding down the left hand mouse button**.

8 When your picture is shown as selected **click** on **File** at the top right hand side of the **Menu bar**. Scroll down to **Print** with the cursor and click with the left hand mouse button. Your picture and text will now be printed.

9 Using the information in the text, carefully write a title for your printed picture. Neatly add several sentences about Ramesses II in Nubia that you have researched from the text, so that your work can be added to a class display about Ancient Egypt.

Task 2 :
How to find out more about how the rich jewels of the Pharaohs of Ancient Egypt were made, and how to print pictures of a necklace being made.

Check that the **Internet** page with the Address Box is on your screen

1 Delete any address that is in the address box.

2 Type in *www.ancientegypt.co.uk*

3 Now either click on the address box or press the return key.

4 A picture of a lotus flower will open on your screen. Move your cursor over the word **Trades** at the left hand side of the screen and click with your mouse.

5 Read this then click on word **Explore** at the bottom of the screen. A picture of a jewellery necklace will appear. Click on the picture.

6 A picture of men at work in an Ancient Egyptian jewellery workshop will appear. Study this carefully then move the cursor over one of the objects one of the men is holding, click with the left hand mouse button and a detailed picture and text will appear.

7 Make sure your printer is switched on, then **highlight** the picture, with some text that accompanies it, by dragging the cursor over it **holding down the left hand mouse button**.

8 When your picture is shown as selected **click on File** at the top right hand side of the **Menu bar**. Scroll down to **Print** with the cursor and click with the left hand mouse button. Your picture and text will now be printed.

9 Using the information in the text, carefully write a title for your printed picture. Neatly add several sentences about Egyptian Jewellery craftsmen that you have researched from the text, so that your work can be added to a class display about Ancient Egypt.

Task 3

Using a similar method as outlined above research for yourself about mummification, or Egyptian gods and goddesses, or the pyramids so that you can add this research to your Ancient Egyptian display.

Paper and Writing in Ancient Egypt

Task A - A sequencing activity about making Papyrus paper

Carefully study the pictures and information writing showing how the Ancient Egyptians made paper from the papyrus reed. Then cut and paste each picture with its matching text in the correct order on a separate piece of A4 paper to make your own papyrus paper making instruction sheet.

Many of these sheets are then joined together to make a roll of papyrus paper.

The papyrus reed is cut from the banks of the River Nile. Tall young stems are best for making paper.

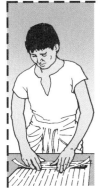

The strips of pith are laid side by side on a flat board.

The outer rind is cut from the young stems of papyrus. The pith inside is cut into strips.

More pith strips are laid at right angles on top of the first set., and then pounded with a wooden mallet. They are left to dry, becoming a stiff sheet of paper.

Task B - Finding out about the past from a range of sources, selecting from your knowledge of history and communicating it in a variety of ways.

Carefully study the Ancient Egyptian writing (called Hieroglyphics) opposite and notice which symbol stands for each letter of our alphabet. Make yourself an Ancient Egyptian obelisk out of card shaped like the Cleopatra's Needle shown down the side of the page. Then create your own hieroglyphic writing for an obelisk. You will have to design hieroglyphs for the letters E, V, X as the Egyptians did not use these letters or sounds.

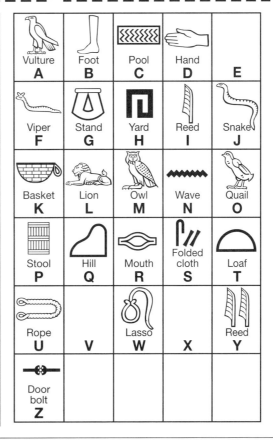

Vulture **A**	Foot **B**	Pool **C**	Hand **D**	**E**
Viper **F**	Stand **G**	Yard **H**	Reed **I**	Snake **J**
Basket **K**	Lion **L**	Owl **M**	Wave **N**	Quail **O**
Stool **P**	Hill **Q**	Mouth **R**	Folded cloth **S**	Loaf **T**
Rope **U**	**V**	Lasso **W**	**X**	Reed **Y**
Door bolt **Z**				

Obelisk

The first picture writing dates from 3100 B.C. There were over 750 different pictures to show letters or sounds or words.

The picture writing was carved on temple walls and needle shaped stones. Later it was carved on clay slabs to record different messages for the Pharaohs. Even later on it came to be written in ink on papyrus paper.

From 700 B.C. the symbols became more like writing. This was called the Demotic Script

Women's Lives in Ancient Egypt

Rich Women

- had many slaves as servants
- went to many rich feasts
- often ran large farms when their husbands were away
- had to share their husband with 1 or 2 more wives
- wore fine white linen dresses
- spent lots of time painting their faces
- showed they were rich by their gold and jewels

Ordinary Women

- wore simple white linen tunic dresses
- had very few personal goods
- made all the family's bread
- cooked all the family meals
- had to help their husbands with work at busy times
- cleaned the home daily
- bartered goods for food in the market
- looked after the children all day long
- spun and wove flax to make the family's clothes
- looked after everything when their husbands were sent away to work for the Pharaoh

Slave Women

- wore simple plain skirts
- were often captured in Egypt's wars
- could be bought and sold
- worked long days for rich people
- could marry and then be free
- could be dancers or play music at feasts
- had few personal goods
- mainly worked as house servants

Women's Rights in Ancient Egypt

Ancient Egypt Women

- were well treated
- could earn wages
- could own houses and land
- could go to court if they were badly treated
- could go where ever they wanted
- could inherit their parents land and goods, if there was no son in the family
- could even become Pharaoh

Ancient Egypt Women Priests

- wore fine white dresses and rich head dresses
- spent three months in the temple then three months at home.
- washed twice a day and twice a night to be pure for the gods in the temple.
- Said prayers for the Pharaoh every day in the temple
- Sang and danced in front of the god's statues
- Made medicines for the sick who came to the temple

Task A - Comparing and Contrasting Historical Evidence

Divide a separate sheet of A4 paper in half down its length. Put a title 'Ordinary Ancient Egyptian Women' at the head of one column and 'Ordinary Modern Women' at the head of the other column. List neatly the tasks an Ancient Egyptian Woman had to do, then in the other column list the tasks an ordinary modern woman has to do in her day. When you have completed your task discuss the similarities and differences with your partner, group or class.

Task B - Interpreting Evidence from Different Sources

Carefully read the statements below and from the evidence on pages 22 and 23 decide whether each statement is **True** or **False** or **There is no evidence** for you to decide. Write a reason for your choice to go with each statement.

1 Rich women in Ancient Egypt worked hard every day.
2 Ancient Egyptian slave women could never be free.
3 There were some Pharaohs in Ancient Egypt who were women.
4 Women Priests in Ancient Egypt were paid a lot of money.
5 Ancient Egyptian women weren't allowed to go to court.
6 Rich Egyptian women often shared their husband with other wives.
7 Many women slaves in Ancient Egypt came from outside Egypt.
8 Ancient Egyptian women were equal to men.
9 Women priests were wonderful dancers.
10 All Egyptian women washed four times a day.

The Gift of The River Nile

The Black Land

(shown darker)

This was the land near the River Nile's banks.

It was called the Black Land because of the rich black soil left behind when the River Nile flooded.

The Red Land

This was the name for the desert in Ancient Egypt. It was called this because it was so hot and dry and the soil was red.

Very few people could live in the Red Land because it was so dry.

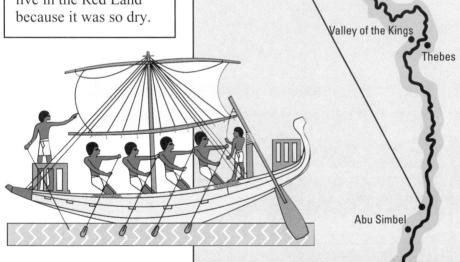

Alexandria

Giza
Memphis

Valley of the Kings

Thebes

Abu Simbel

'Hail to you O Nile , who issues from the Earth and comes to keep Egypt alive'

Hymn to Hapi the Ancient Egyptian god of the Nile.

The Kingdom of Ancient Egypt was very long.

The River Nile was the quickest way to travel about. Boats were made of reeds or wood which grew near the banks of the River Nile. They used oars to row them along or sails to use the wind to move their boats

Task – A Reasoning Exercise

1 Why do you think the Ancient Egyptians sang hymns to the god Hapi?
2 Why do you think the land near the River Nile was called the Black Land?
3 Why do you think the Ancient Egyptians called some land The Red Land?
4 How did the Ancient Egyptians move their boats on the River Nile?
5 What gifts is Hapi the god of the Nile shown giving to the Ancient Egyptians?
6 Why do you think the cities of Ancient Egypt were built away from the banks of the Nile?
7 Why do you think that the Ancient Egyptians built their boats from reeds or wood?
8 List all the gifts the River Nile gave to the people of Ancient Egypt?
9 Research in reference books to find out how the Ancient Egyptians got food from the River Nile.

The Seasons of the Nile

Life in Ancient Egypt was ruled by what was happening to the River Nile. The people's lives changed throughout each year to fit in with the changes in the height of the waters of the River Nile.

September

As the Nile water rises lots more fish are swept down the river. Men catch these fish from reed boats on the banks of the River Nile.

The end of July

The Nile begins to rise. It is the end of the harvest season. People go to the temple to give thanks for the harvest, and the gift of the River Nile.

November

As the flood waters go down, the farmers go back to their lands near the River Nile. They plough up the rich soil left by the floods.

August

The River Nile waters are high. The harvest is over. Many men are sent to work on building the Pharaoh's temples and palaces.

January to March

It is the hot dry time. The farmers have to get water from the Nile. They use a shaduf to get the water from the Nile to their fields.

October

The River Nile flood is at its highest. Each village and town marks its height on a special marker stone. It is called a Nilometer.

March

The corn is ready to harvest. Many people come to help the farmers gather in the corn. It will be stored so that the people can have bread for the next year.

Late September

As the River Nile floods, the people move to their homes on higher land away from the River Nile.

June

The farmers now harvest the dates, grapes, olives and vegetables. Many people help the farmers.

December

The farmers plant the seeds for all their crops in the rich new soil brought to their lands by the River Nile floods.

Task - Chronological Order

The facts about the River Nile in Ancient Egyptian times above have been mixed up. Cut them out and paste them in the correct chronological order on a fresh piece of paper.

Food and Drink in Ancient Egypt

Beer

Made from mashed stale bread Ancient Egyptian beer needed to be strained through holes in the wooden mouthpiece of this beer strainer.

Bread

This loaf is over 3,000 years old. It was found next to a buried Mummy. The bread has bits of grit in it. Archaeologists think that this would have made the teeth of Ancient Egyptians wear out quickly.

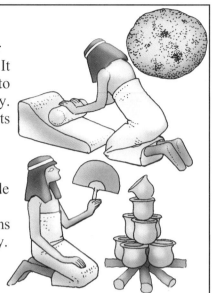

Beef

This model tells us that beef was a common meat eaten by the Ancient Egyptians. Archaeologists have found skewers with beef pieces on them, telling us that they barbecued meat.

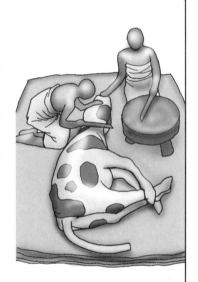

Onions and Leeks

Archaeologists tell us that the Ancient Egyptians put baskets of food in the tombs of rich people. They thought it would feed the person in their after life. Dried up leeks and onions have been found in these baskets.

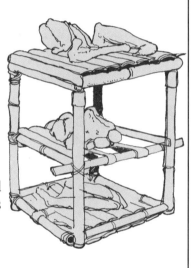

Fish

This engraving was found on a casket in the Tomb of Tutankhamun. It shows villagers catching fish for their meals. Fish bones have also been found in pots in tombs.

Wine

These men are treading grapes to make into wine. Archaeologists have found pottery wine jars in many tombs in Egypt.

Food and Drink in Ancient Egypt

Fruit

Dried up pieces of fruit found in tomb chambers tell archaeologists that the Ancient Egyptians had a healthy fruit diet which would give them lots of vitamins.

Geese

These men are shown herding geese to the Pharaoh's kitchens. This picture was found by archaeologists on a temple wall at Thebes.

Hunting

The rich would have hunting expeditions into the desert. Wall paintings show them returning with deer, gazelles and desert hares to eat.

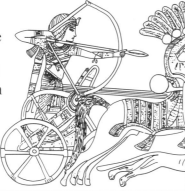

Bees

Model bee hives have been found in many tombs telling archaeologists that this was the way Ancient Egyptians used honey to sweeten food.

Task A - Using evidence from pages 26 and 27

1   What evidence tells you that the Ancient Egyptians had a problem with their teeth?

2   Why do you think the Ancient Egyptians drank their beer through a strainer?

3   What evidence tells you that the Ancient Egyptians had plenty of vitamins in their diet?

4. Why do you think that the rich Ancient Egyptians went hunting in the desert?

5   Which evidence tells us that the Ancient Egyptians drank wine?

6   Why do you think archaeologists can say that the Ancient Egyptians cooked their meat over a sort of barbecue?

7   List the different types of meat this evidence tells you that the Ancient Egyptians ate.

8   Examine the evidence carefully again, then say which sort of archaeological site gives most evidence to archaeologists about the Ancient Egyptians food and drinking habits?

Task B - Presenting Information in a Different Ways

Using the information on pages 26 and 27 make up a day's menu card for a rich Ancient Egyptian family.

Conduct a survey of your class or friends to find their top ten favourite Ancient Egyptian foods.

Task C - Taking the Topic Further

Research in reference books to find other foods and drinks that the Ancient Egyptians ate.

The Ancient Egyptians at War

Carefully study the pictures on page 28, and the text on page 29. Cut out and paste each group of weapons on separate sheets of paper. Add your own text next to each picture, explaining what each weapon was made of, who used it and how it was used.

Weapons used by the Ancient Egyptian Army

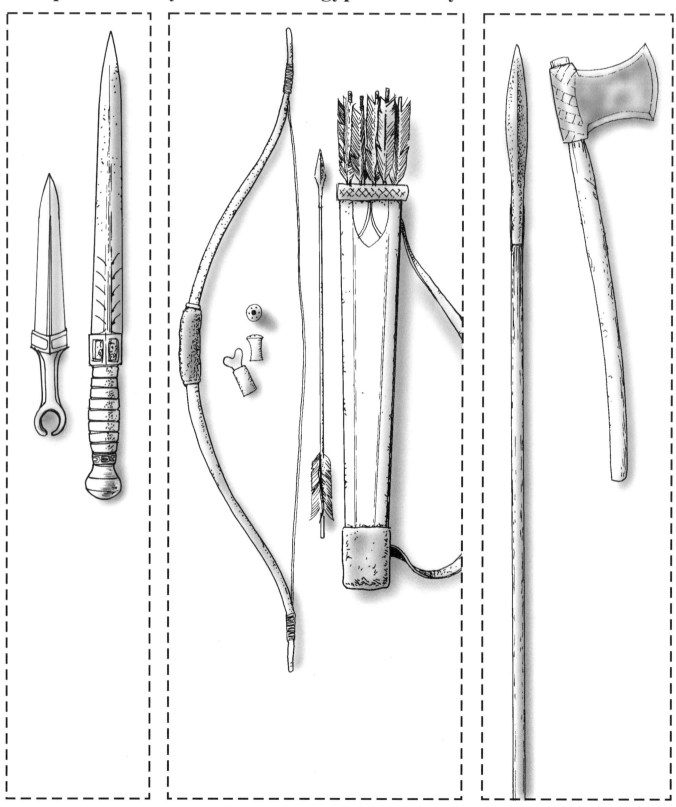

The Ancient Egyptians at War

Who did the fighting?

There were men on foot with shields, spears, axes and slings. There were pairs of men in chariots pulled by horses, with one man steering and one man firing arrows or throwing spears.

What did they wear?

Most men in the army wore a skirt and sandals. Officers wore armour made of thick leather with pieces of metal to make it stronger. Sometimes a rich officer would wear a helmet.

Why did they fight?

They fought because men from another country wanted the rich things the Egyptians had. Sometimes the Egyptians wanted gold, silver and other rich things found in other countries.

What were the weapons made from?

The spears, arrows and axes had heads of flint, hard wood, or bronze. The shafts of the axes, spears and arrrows were made of wood. The swords and daggers were made from a metal called bronze.

How did the soldiers use the weapons?

The soldiers rode close to the enemy on their chariots and then fired their arrows. Spears were thrown at the enemy from a distance. The soldiers got very close to the enemy to fight with axes, swords and daggers.

Task B

Carefully study the picture on page 29. Write an imaginary short section of dialogue between the foot soldiers and the chariot warriors as they prepare to go into battle.

The Ancient Egyptians at War

The Egyptian Army camp on their way to battle.

Priests prayed for the soldiers.

Scribes wrote down what happened to the soldiers.

Doctors looked after the soldiers wounds.

Task:

Carefully study the picture and the text. Imagine you are a scribe with the Egyptian army. Write a description of the army camp which has been set up on the way to fight a battle.

How did they keep the camp safe?

They dug a ditch all the way around their camp. They made a wall with their shields all around the camp. They put guards at the gateway of the camp.

Who went with the soldiers?

Scribes went to write down what happened. Doctors went to look after the soldiers' wounds. A priest went with the soldiers to pray for the soldiers.

Where did they sleep in the camp?

The officers, scribes and doctors slept in tents on folding beds. The soldiers slept outside on reed mats.

THE
GREAT PYRAMID ROBBERY GAME

THE AIM OF THE GAME

You are an Ancient Egyptian tomb robber. You meet a builder from the Great Pyramid in a Giza beer house. He tells you the way into the pyramid and where the rich treasure lies inside. You have to get into the Pyramid, visit the Queen's and the Pharaoh's tomb rooms, take a piece of treasure from each, then return to the Giza beer house.

BACKGROUND

For up to 4 players.

The Ancient Egyptians thought that they needed to take many things from this life into the 'next life' after they died. As a result, their tombs were filled with rooms full of rich goods.

The Pharaoh Kufu and his Queen were buried in a tomb inside the Great Pyramid at Giza about 2550 B.C. They had many very rich objects buried with them.

Guards were placed around the tombs to prevent people breaking in and robbing the rich things from the tomb.

Occasionally, tomb robbers would break into the pyramid and steal all the Pharaoh's and their Queen's riches.

YOU WILL NEED

- A dice
- A shaker
- Each player needs a playing piece
- The Pharaoh's Treasure and the Queen's Treasure in the correct Tomb Room.

HOW TO PLAY THE GAME

Your teacher sets a time limit for your game.

1 Before you start playing the game place the Pharaoh's treasure in the King's tomb room, and the Queen's treasure in the Queen's tomb room.

2 Each player throws the dice once, the player with the highest number chooses their playing piece and starts the game first. Other players follow in order of their dice throws.

3 Each player starts in the Giza beer house. They have to throw a 6 to start as this stands for the time they are getting information from the pyramid builder. Each player follows in turn.

4 Once a six is thrown then another number is thrown and the player moves their playing piece that number of places along the numbered route to the Pyramid and inside the Pyramid. Other players follow in turn.

5 All players landing on a space with instructions must follow the instructions exactly.

6 When a player lands in the Queen's tomb room, they throw a dice until they get a number that matches the treasure left in the room. They can only throw the dice once when it is their turn.

7 When any player lands in the Pharaoh's tomb room they must follow the same rules as the Queen's tomb room to get their Pharaoh's treasure.

8 When any player arrives in the lower tomb room they must throw a 6 to get out. This stands for the time the robbers spent searching in the dark.

9 The winner is the first player to have visited all three tomb rooms and return to the Giza beer house with two pieces of treasure.

The Playing Pieces

HIPPO MONKEY HAWK SNAKE

The Pharaoh's Treasure

Mask 1 Chest 2 Necklace 3 Staff 4

The Queen's Treasure

Mask 1 Crown 2 Necklace 3 Pendant 4

THE GREAT PYRAMID

Menkawre

Ancient Egyptian Tomb Robbers

Robbers getting away

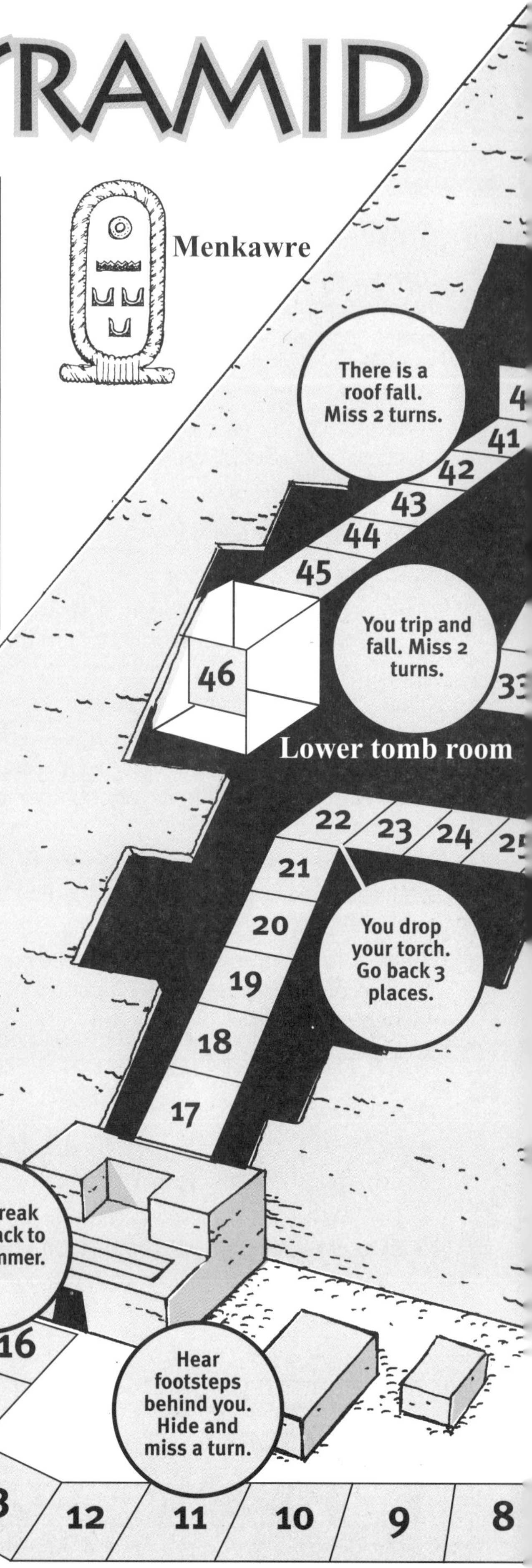

There is a roof fall. Miss 2 turns.

4

41

42

43

44

45

46

You trip and fall. Miss 2 turns.

33

Lower tomb room

22 / 23 / 24 / 25

21

20

19

18

17

You drop your torch. Go back 3 places.

Can't break in. Go back to 3 for hammer.

16

15

14

13

Hear footsteps behind you. Hide and miss a turn.

12   11   10   9   8

ROBBERY GAME

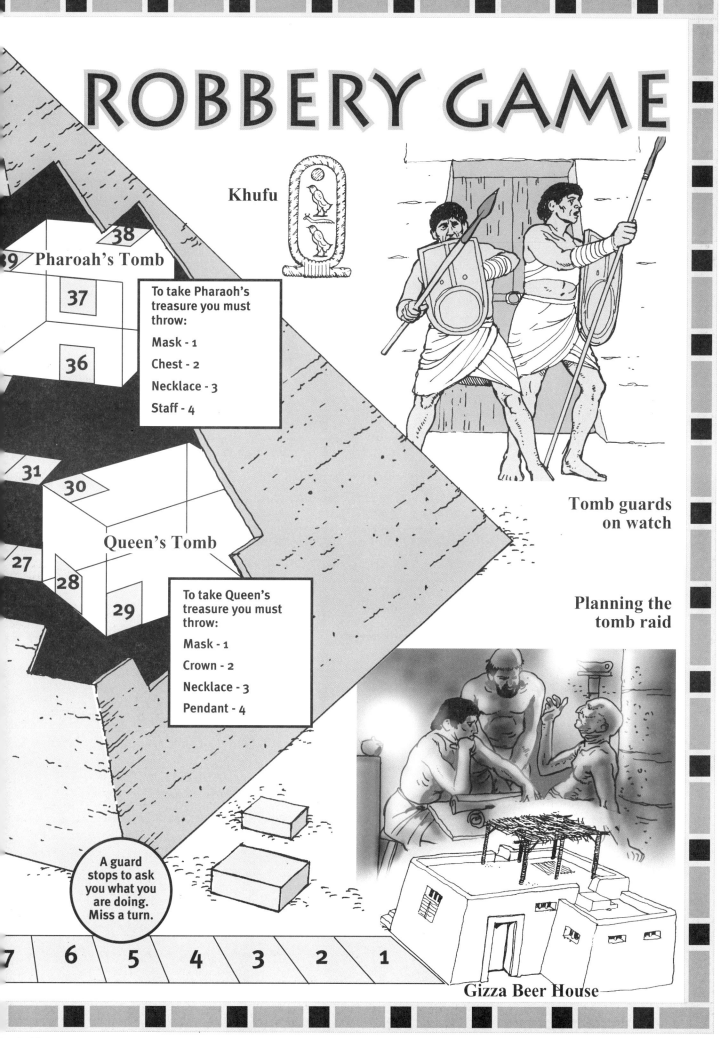

Khufu

39 **Pharoah's Tomb**
38
37
36

To take Pharaoh's treasure you must throw:

Mask - 1
Chest - 2
Necklace - 3
Staff - 4

Tomb guards on watch

31
30

Queen's Tomb

27
28
29

To take Queen's treasure you must throw:

Mask - 1
Crown - 2
Necklace - 3
Pendant - 4

Planning the tomb raid

A guard stops to ask you what you are doing. Miss a turn.

7 **6** **5** **4** **3** **2** **1**

Gizza Beer House

Cleopatra - the last Ruler of Ancient Egypt

Task A - Write a Biography

Research, in reference books, to find out as much information as you can about Cleopatra. Then continue the biography and character sketch of Cleopatra which has been started for you here.

Alexander the Great, the King of Greece, attacked Egypt in 332 B.C. His Greek family ruled Egypt from then on. They made Egypt like Greece. The Pharaohs now spoke Greek. All the Pharaohs were now called Ptolemy. They kept the Ancient Egyptian gods but added Greek gods and customs. When Pharaoh Ptolemy XII died in 51 B.C., Cleopatra who was only seventeen years old, ruled Egypt with her younger brother, Ptolemy XIII. But Cleopatra did not want to share the crown of Egypt, she wanted to rule Egypt on her own. So…

Make an Ancient Egyptian 'Magazine'

Task : Be a Magazine Editor for a Day

On this page you have two articles plus pictures from your illustrators. Complete the next two pages ready for your magazine's printing. Cut out and paste under your sub-editor's suggested titles the articles on this page. Notice that there are some story lines and pictures missing. As print day is tomorrow you will have to research, draw and write these items yourself to fill the empty column space. All the subtitles you need are provided for you.

As you stroll about the temple you will meet priests and priestesses leading sacred animals about. You will find some of these animals sitting in cages near to the god or goddess with whom they are linked.

On a recent visit I saw a sacred cat with a gold ring through its nose in a gold cage next to the god Bastet. People were saying prayers to her hoping she would bring the sun to shine on their crops.

Our artist's drawing of a procession of priests entering the magnificent temple to the god Osiris at Thebes, Lower Egypt.

Our illustrators picture of Anubis, god of the dead and embalming, helping prepare a mummy for burial.

Thousands of people come to worship by the figure of Thoth, the Ibis headed god of the moon. They are hoping that he will grant them power in their writing, music, building and mathematics.

Thoth is the favourite god of scribes, painters and builders. They bring offerings to lay at the god's feet.

The god has the head of the Ibis bird found fishing the Nile and the irrigation canals by night. Its curved beak is a symbol of the crescent moon.

The wisdom of Thoth is said to come from the moon.

GODS AND GODDESSES MONTHLY

SACRED ANIMALS LIVE IN THE TEMPLES

Draw your own illustration of a sacred temple cat here

ANUBIS – THE GOD WHO HELPS YOU INTO THE NEXT WORLD

Our illustrators picture of Anubis, god of the dead and embalming, helping prepare a mummy for burial.

OSIRIS – THE GREATEST OF THE GODS OF EGYPT

GODS AND GODDESSES MONTHLY

THOTH - THE GOD OF MOON, A GREAT TEACHER GOD

PRIESTS AND PRIESTESSES THE KEEPERS OF THE TEMPLE

Our artist's drawing of a procession of priests entering the magnificent temple to the god Osiris at Thebes, Lower Egypt.

BES THE FUN LOVING GOD OF CHILDREN AND THE HOME

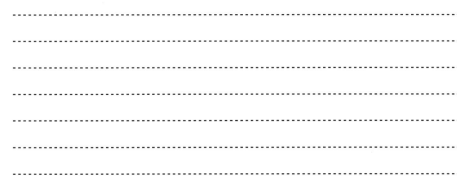

Write a Pharaoh's Diary

Facts about Pharaohs

- The Pharaohs were the rulers of Egypt.
- A Pharaoh was the most important person in Ancient Egypt.
- The Pharaoh owned all the land of Egypt.
- The Pharaoh had to be a great warrior to fight Egypt's enemies.
- The people of Egypt thought that the Pharaoh was a living God.
- The people of Egypt would give rich gifts to the Pharaohs.

- The Pharaohs travelled up and down the River Nile in very large boats.
- Some of the favourite pastimes of the Pharaohs were hunting and fishing.
- The Pharaohs led special services in the temples of Ancient Egypt.
- Some Pharaohs were women.
- The word Pharaoh means great house.
- The Pharaohs were buried with many rich gifts.

Task - Using information to write in a diary style.

Read carefully the facts on this page and the start to the Pharaoh's diary. Research in reference works further information about the Pharaoh's lives. Use your imagination to complete the diary which has been started below.

Day 1

I awoke early, I was excited as I had planned a great hunt in the desert for lions, deer, and wild horses. First I was rowed down the Nile in my fast moving barge. I came back on land in an area where the wild creatures had been seen recently. My gold chariot was waiting

....

....

....

....

....

....

....

....

....

....

....

....

....

....

Make your own 3D Pharaoh's Feast

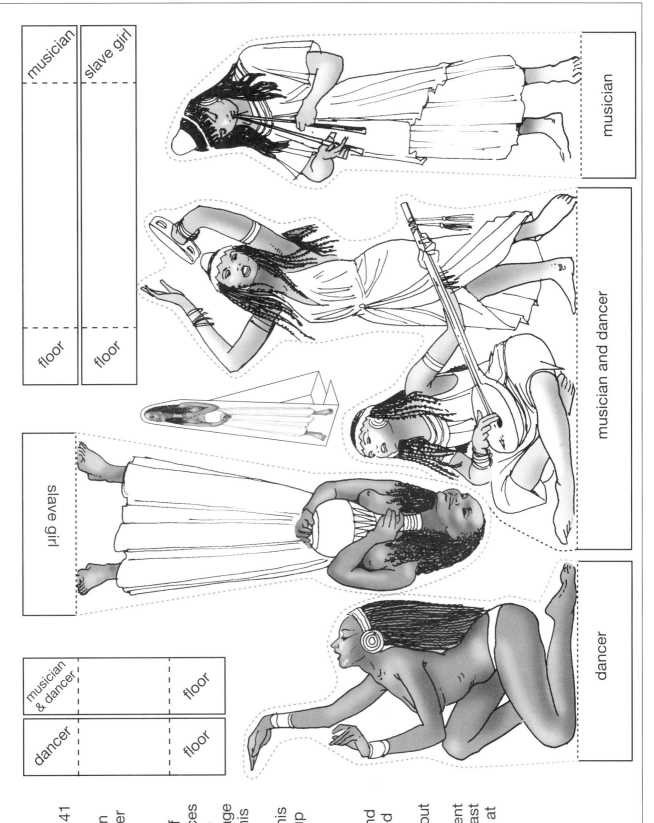

musician	slave girl

floor	floor

slave girl

musician & dancer	dancer
floor	floor

musician

musician and dancer

dancer

Instructions

1. Copy pages 39, 40 and 41 onto thin card.

2. Use masking tape to join pages 40 and 41 together as indicated.

3. Research in reference books to find pictures of feasts in Pharaoh's palaces then carefully colour the palace background on page 40, and the figures on this page.

4. Cut out the figures on this page. Fold the shapes up along their dotted lines. Paste the strips to the figures and the floor.

5. Research in books to find details of what happened at an Egptian feast.

6. Write your own report about the food and drink, the dancing and entertainment and the people at the feast at the Pharaoh's palace at Thebes.

Pharaoh's Feast

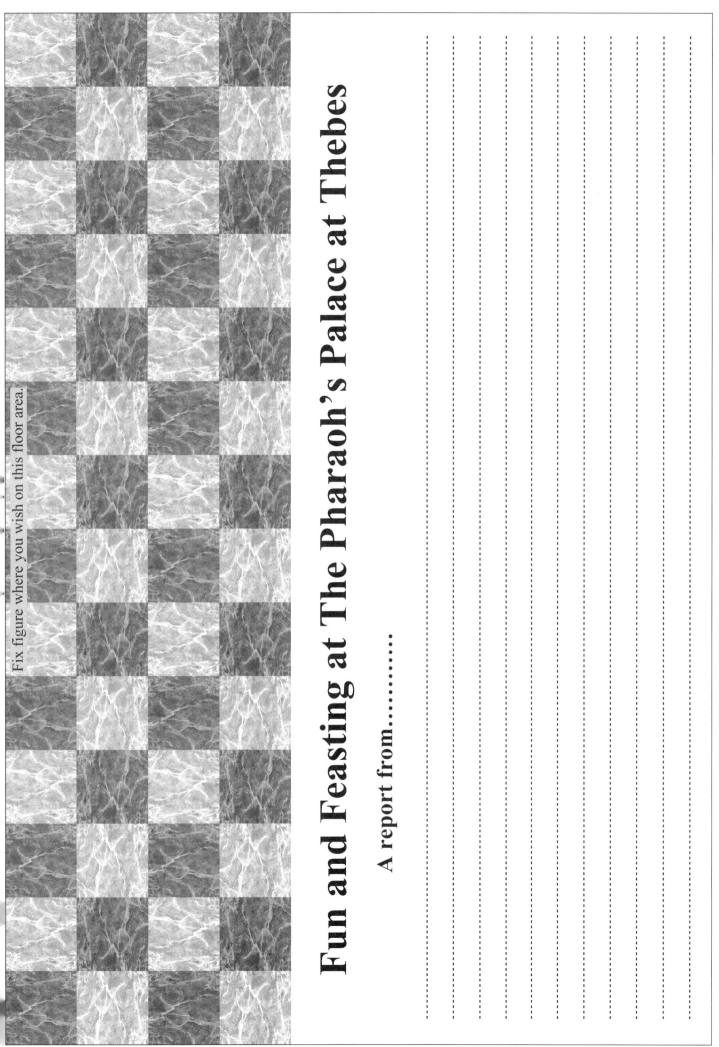

Fix figure where you wish on this floor area.

Fun and Feasting at The Pharaoh's Palace at Thebes

A report from...........

Ancient Egyptian Wall Decorations

The Ancient Egyptians loved to cover the walls of their temples and palaces with panels of brightly painted sculptures and hieroglyphic writings. These pictures often told about the lives of the Pharaohs or the acts of their gods and goddesses. They are full of the actions of animals, birds and people.

Task A

In the three wall panels above, continue the decoration, drawing over the faint lines to complete the designs

Task B

Now colour your patterns carefully. Use the Ancient Egyptians favourite colours of red, blue, yellow and green.

Task C

Search for other Ancient Egyptian wall decorations in reference books and make your own collection.

Instructions for Making Models
See finished models on page 64

General

Ideally, photocopy the sheets onto thin card rather than paper. Cream coloured card can make more attractive models. Some models will look better, and will be easier to make, if enlarged. (A4 up to A3 for example)

If you wish to colour the models, it is better to colour the pieces before cutting them out. Coloured pencils or crayons are preferable to water paint, which will tend to warp and soften the paper or card.

Cut out along the solid black lines. Score along the dotted lines before folding. Use 'PrittStick' or PVA glue to fix. Ideally, test pieces together before gluing.

Mummy Case (page 47)

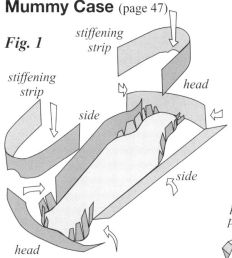

Fig. 1

This is a simple model in 3 pieces. It looks very good coloured. Use blue, red and green. Gild with a gold pen.

First, assemble the basic case. (see diagram, *Fig. 1*). Finally, fix stiffening strips inside the head and foot of the case, with the dimple inside the case. Children might be paired off to make two cases (one to fit inside the other, as in box and lid). If you want to do this child B's model could be slightly smaller (say 98%). Use different coloured card for the smaller box and the larger lid.

Pyramid (pages 48 and 49)

This model will benefit from being photocopied larger. This is a simple model in just 3 pieces. The finished model represents the complete pyramid with a removable segment, revealing the interior of the pyramid. The actual pyramid was made from white limestone. Originally, the apex of the pyramid would have been coated with gold. White card would be more corect.

First cut out and assemble the largest part. See diagram (*Fig. 2*). Next cut out the small square piece and place on the exposed area

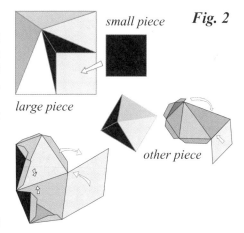

small piece **Fig. 2**

large piece

other piece

of base. Finally, assemble the remaining piece to form the removable segment. Note that a legend has been provided to explain the letters on the model. Children might write this out and place next to their model pyramid.

Sphinx (pages 46 and 49)

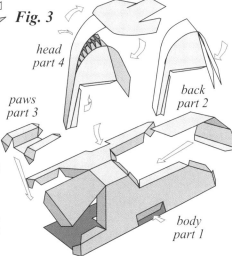

Fig. 3

head part 4

paws part 3

back part 2

body part 1

This is a more complex model. Parts are on pages 46 and 49. Study the picture of the finished model and see the diagram (*Fig. 3*). First, cut out and assemble the main body of the sphinx. The cut-out in the base is to allow fingers inside the model, to ease assembly. Next, cut out and fix part 2. This forms the back of the sphinx. Note the faint words on the piece to aid correct alignment. Now, cut out and fix part 3. This fits between the front legs and forms the fore limbs and paws of the sphinx. Note the faint words (paws). Finally, cut out carefully, and fix part 4. This is the tricky piece, and forms the head. Study separate diagram (*fig. 3 - head part 4*) before fixing head.

Boat (pages 44 and 45)

This model looks more complex than it is. Study the diagram (*Fig. 5*) before you begin.

Parts are on pages 44 and 45.

Start by cutting out the hull, the deck and the base. Accurate scoring and folding is very important. Study the diagram (fig. 4). First, join the two sides together. The white bow and stern sections fit under the decorated part on the other side. Next, fix the joined sides to the base. The base has shaded areas to assist correct alignment. Before fixing deck ensure that the cut-out centre has been removed, including the small cut-out for the mast. When hull is dry, fix deck on to the hull. It does not matter which way round the deck is fitted, but once fitted the bow and stern have been determined.

First, join the two sides together. The white bow and stern sections fit under the decorated part on the other side.

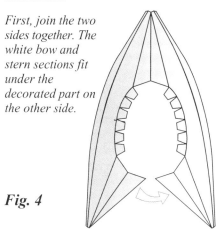

Fig. 4

The second stage completes the boat. Cut out the remaining 6 pieces. Fold and glue the rudder, and put aside. Fold and glue the mast, and put aside. Carefully score the sail and fold. Carefully cut out the two small holes which allow the sail to be threaded onto the mast.

Final assembly. Bend the shelter into an arch shape and fix to base of boat, after passing through the opening in the deck. Fix mast in front of the shelter and fix to base, though opening in deck. Thread the sail down over the mast until the bottom of the sail is in line with the top of the shelter. Fix the rudder to the starboard (right-hand) side of the boat at the stern, See Diagram (fig 5). Finally fold and fix bow and stern posts.

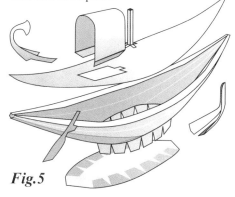

Fig.5

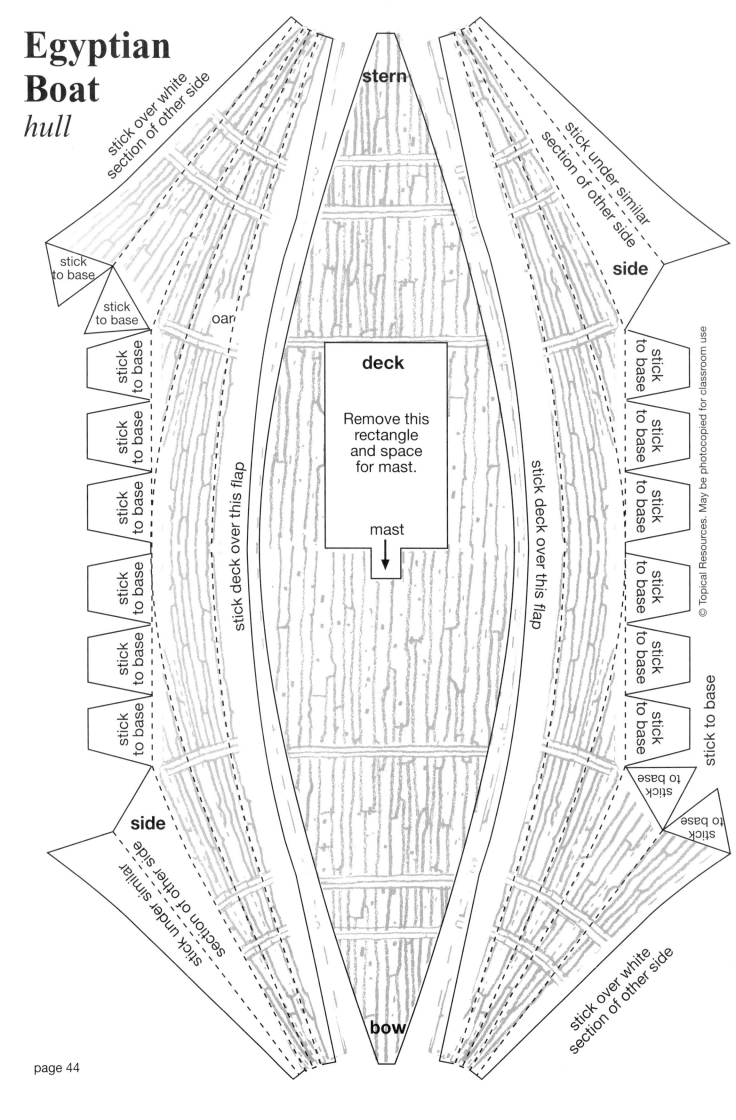

Egyptian Boat
hull

stick over white section of other side

stern

stick to base

stick to base

stick to base

stick to base

stick to base

stick to base

stick to base

stick to base

oar

stick deck over this flap

deck

Remove this rectangle and space for mast.

mast

stick under similar section of other side

side

stick to base
stick to base
stick to base
stick to base
stick to base
stick to base

© Topical Resources. May be photocopied for classroom use

stick deck over this flap

stick to base

stick to base

stick to base

side

stick under similar section of other side

bow

stick over white section of other side

Egyptian Boat: *other parts*

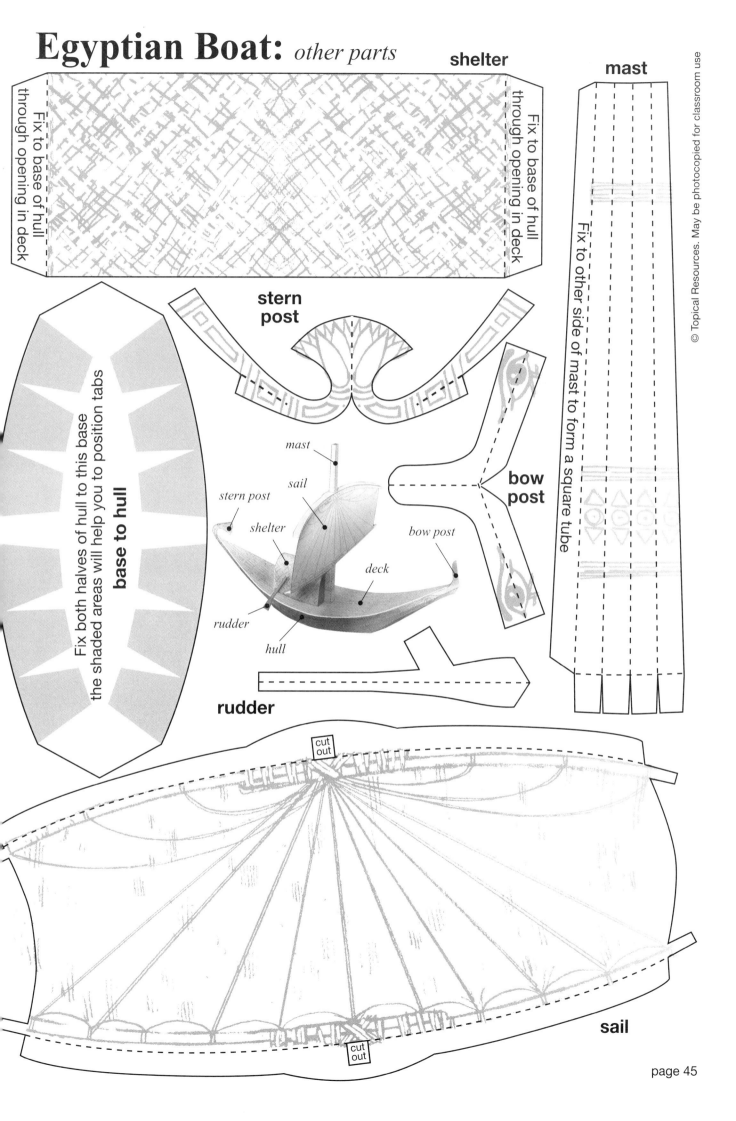

shelter

Fix to base of hull through opening in deck

Fix to base of hull through opening in deck

mast

Fix to other side of mast to form a square tube

stern post

bow post

base to hull

Fix both halves of hull to this base the shaded areas will help you to position tabs

mast

sail

stern post

shelter

bow post

deck

rudder

hull

rudder

cut out

cut out

sail

Sphinx
Main body

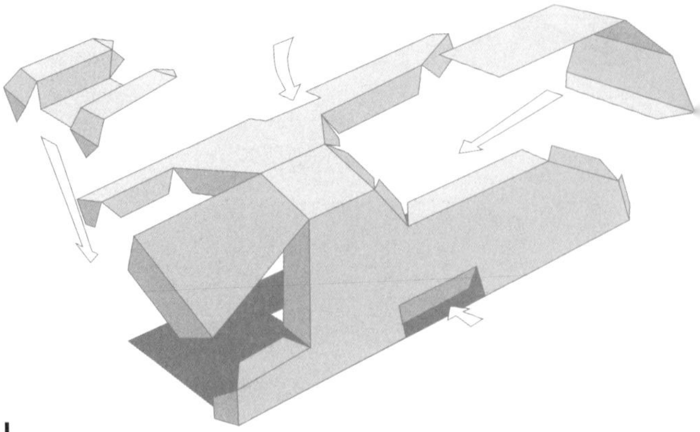

cut 3 sides of flap and fold to create recess under

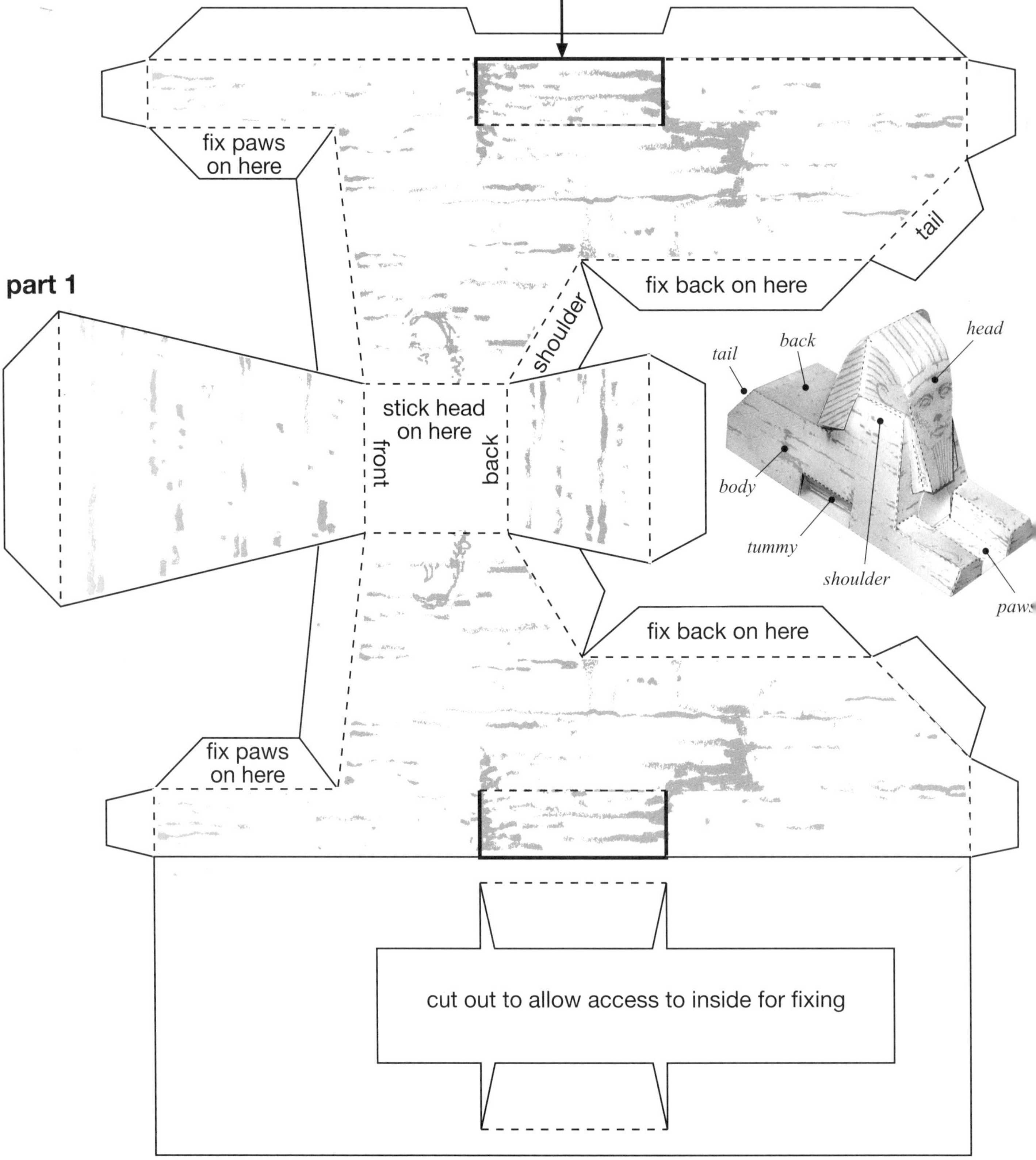

part 1

fix paws
on here

tail

fix back on here

shoulder

stick head
on here

front

back

back

tail

head

body

tummy

shoulder

paws

fix back on here

fix paws
on here

cut out to allow access to inside for fixing

other pieces on page 49

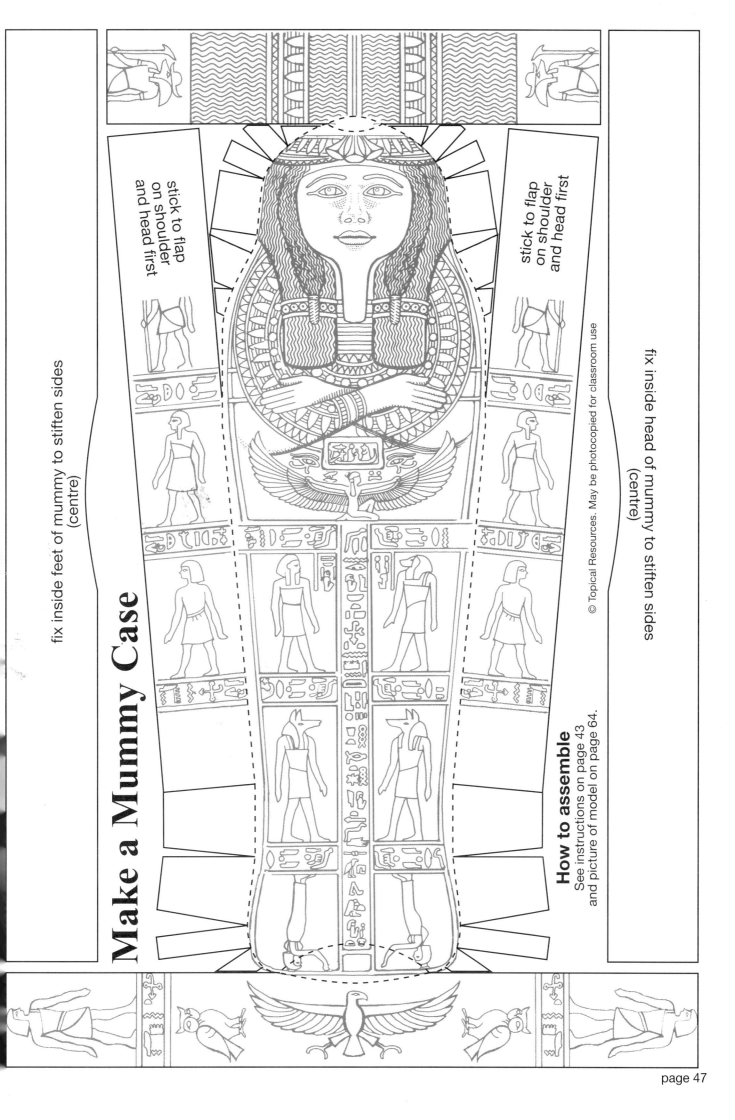

Make a Mummy Case

fix inside feet of mummy to stiffen sides
(centre)

stick to flap
on shoulder
and head first

stick to flap
on shoulder
and head first

fix inside head of mummy to stiffen sides
(centre)

How to assemble
See instructions on page 43
and picture of model on page 64.

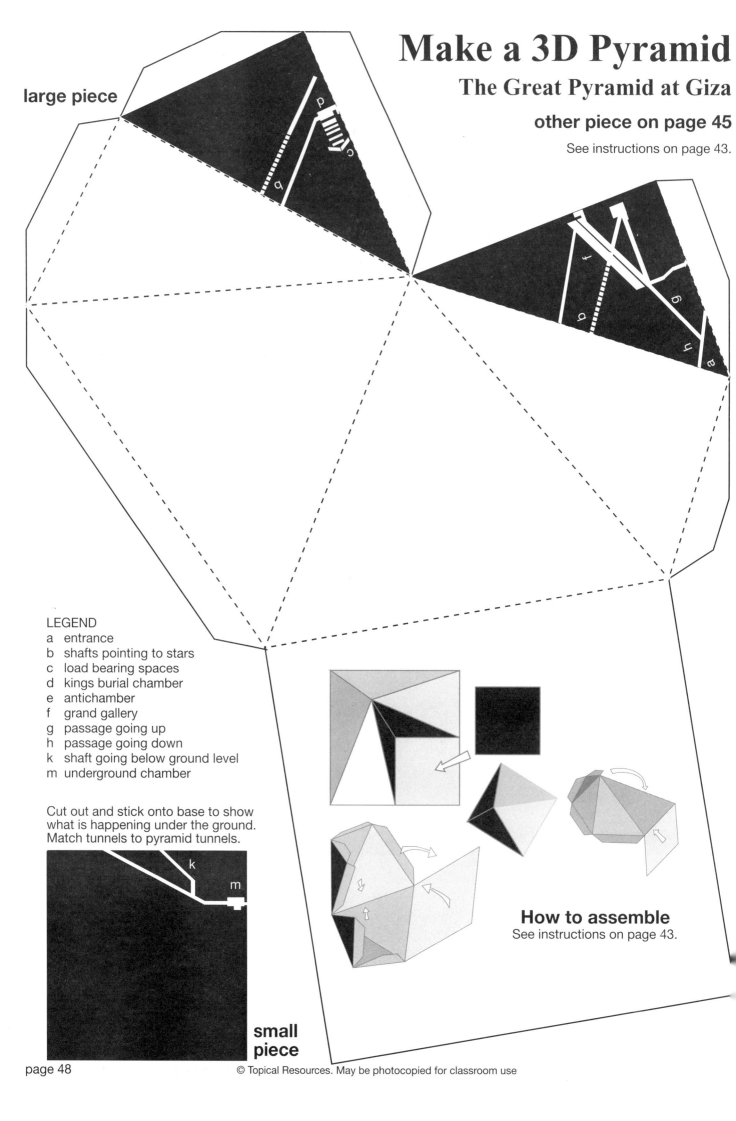

Make a 3D Pyramid
The Great Pyramid at Giza

other piece on page 45

See instructions on page 43.

large piece

LEGEND
a entrance
b shafts pointing to stars
c load bearing spaces
d kings burial chamber
e antichamber
f grand gallery
g passage going up
h passage going down
k shaft going below ground level
m underground chamber

Cut out and stick onto base to show what is happening under the ground. Match tunnels to pyramid tunnels.

small piece

How to assemble
See instructions on page 43.

Pyramid
other parts

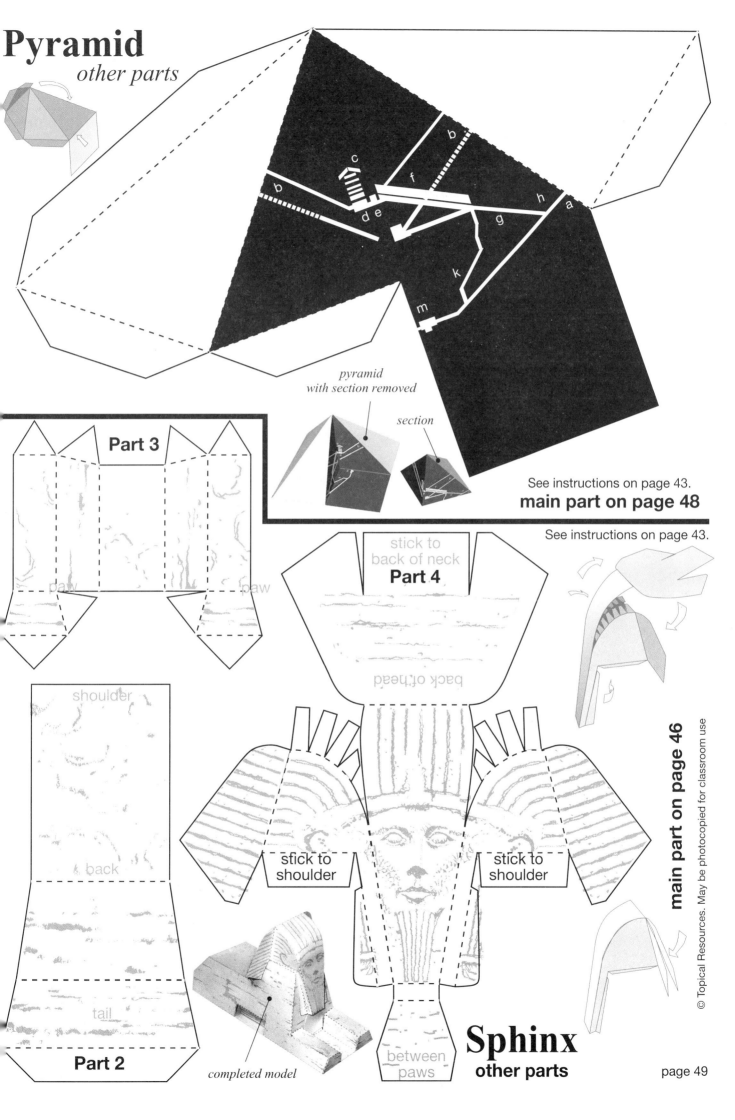

*pyramid
with section removed*

section

See instructions on page 43.
main part on page 48

See instructions on page 43.

Part 3

paw

paw

Part 4

stick to
back of neck

back of head

shoulder

back

stick to
shoulder

stick to
shoulder

tail

Part 2

completed model

between
paws

Sphinx
other parts

main part on page 46

How to make an Ancient Egyptian Mummy

Task A - Putting Historical Events into Chronological Order

The story of how the Ancient Egyptians made a mummy have been mixed up on pages 50 and 51. Carefully study the pictures and text on these pages, then cut out each section separately and paste it in the correct order on a separate piece of A4 paper.

Finally the wrapped and decorated body, with its gold mask, was placed inside a human shaped wooden coffin. Magic spells were said by the priest, who was wearing a 'Mask of Anubis' the god of the dead. Then the wooden coffin was sealed with wax.

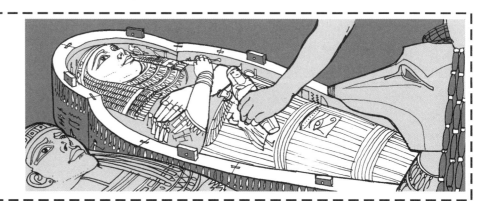

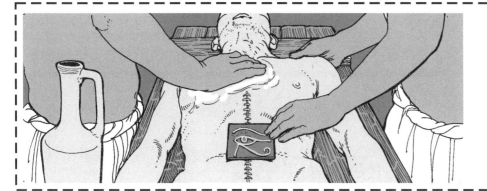

After the 40 days drying out the hole in the body was covered with a lucky Eye of Horus charm to ward off evil spirits. Then oils smelling of perfume were rubbed into the dry skin of the body. This softened and preserved the body.

First the trained men, called embalmers, washed the dead person's body with sweet - smelling palm oil. Whilst they were doing this, a priest read prayers from the 'Book of the Dead', to protect the dead person on his or her journey to the 'next world'.

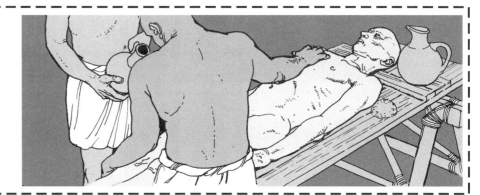

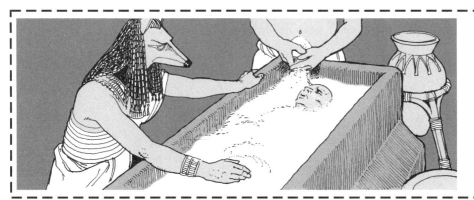

Following the removal of all the inside organs, the body was put in a bath of natron to dry out. The insides of the body were filled with linen cloth, and sand or saw dust. It took forty days for the natron to dry out the body.

How to make an Ancient Egyptian Mummy

Secondly, the brain was pulled out of the head, bit by bit, using a long bronze hook. It was dried in a sort of salt called natron. Then it was covered in a special gum from a tree, bandaged up and put in a pottery storage jar. The jar had a top shaped like one of the gods of Ancient Egypt.

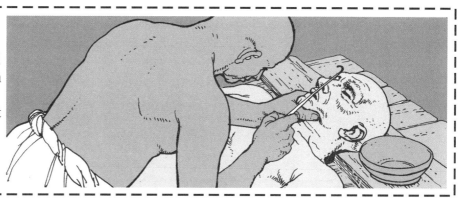

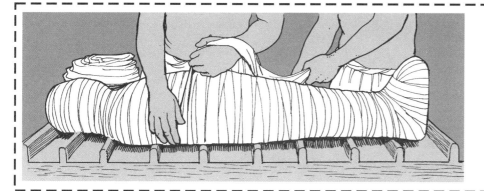

Once the hole in the body had been sealed, the whole body was wrapped in layers of linen bandages. Lucky charms, to help the body on its journey to the 'next world', were placed in between the layers of bandage.

When the bandaging of the body was complete, a mask of gold and jewels was made. It was placed over the head and shoulders of the body. The mask's face was made to look like the person who had died.

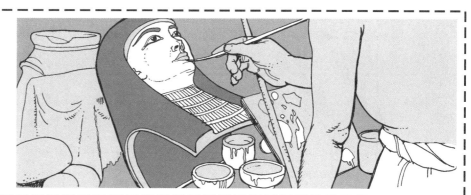

Following the wrapping of the brain, the intestines, the liver, lungs and stomach were cut out. They were dried in natron, then covered with gum, bandaged and put in jars like the brain had been.

Task B – Researching Skills Exercise

Research in reference books to find as many different 'mummy-masks' as you can. Either sketch or photo-copy them. Cut out your work and paste it onto separate pieces of A4 paper to make your own 'mummy-mask' collection.

Snake - an Ancient Egyptian Board Game

The dice has been marked with Ancient Egyptian number symbols.

1= **I**   2= **II**   3= **III**   4= **II II**   5= **II III**   6= **III III**

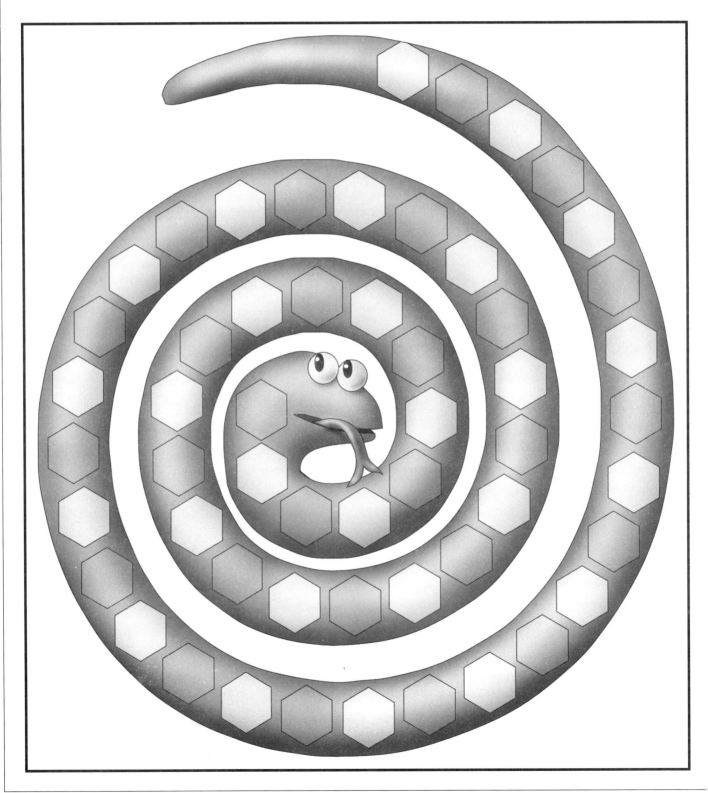

Snake - an Ancient Egyptian Board Game

The Dice

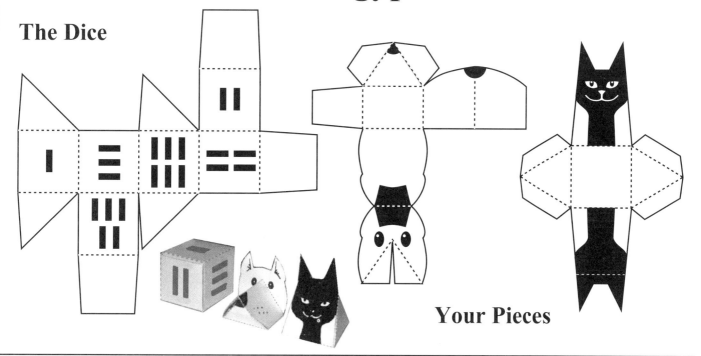

Your Pieces

How to play the Ancient Egyptian Snake Game - for two players

1 Both players roll the dice in turn, the player who gets the highest score starts the game and has first choice of which piece to play with.

2 Each player rolls the dice in turn. A six must be thrown before you can start your piece moving around the snake's body.

3 Each player then rolls the dice, moving their piece around the snake's spiralling body until they reach the head.

4 The correct number on the dice must be rolled to finally reach the snake's head.

5 The winner is the first player to reach the snake's head .

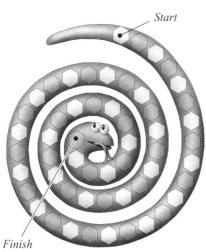

Start

Finish

The Snake Goddess Wadjet

The Cobra Snake appears on the Pharaoh's crown. The Pharaoh was thought then to be protected by the goddess Wadjet from attack by any enemy from behind him. The Cobra goddess on the Crown showed that the Pharaoh would protect The Kingdom of Lower Egypt.

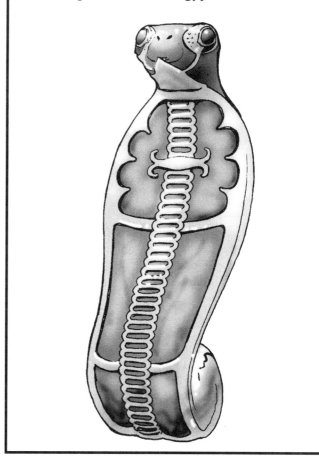

Make an Ancient Egyptian Brooch
Instructional Writing

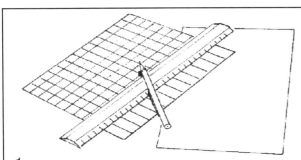

1.

Using a ruler and pencil, divide different coloured pieces of paper into 1 cm squares. You will have to decide how many different colours you want to use in your brooch.

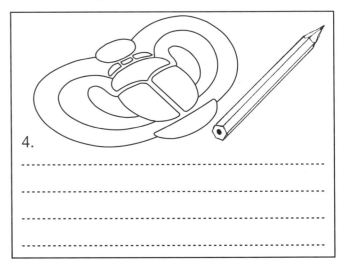

4.

....

....

....

....

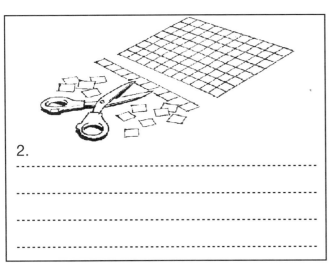

2.

....

....

....

....

5.

Now carefully paste the coloured squares onto the correct places on your brooch design. Work steadily until your design is covered.

3.

Research in reference books to find examples of Ancient Egyptian Brooches. Practice a few different designs on a scrap of paper or a sketch pad. Remember that Ancient Egyptian Brooches were often oval, circular or rectangular in shape.

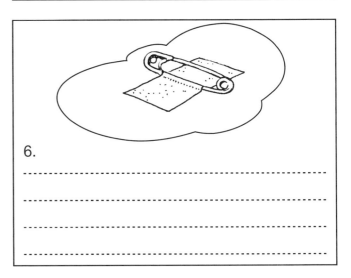

6.

....

....

....

....

Task A

Carefully study the pictures and text about how to make an Ancient Egyptian Brooch. Write your own simple instructions to fill in the missing spaces.

Task B

Now follow your instructions to make your own Ancient Egyptian brooch.

Paint a Pharaoh's Funeral

Task - Paint Your own Pharaoh's Funeral

Research in reference books to find the correct colours when you paint this picture of a Pharaoh's Funeral in Ancient Egypt.

People of Ancient Egypt

The poorest people in Egypt were the slaves. They worked for their masters for no money.

The farmers of Egypt lived near the River Nile. They grew the food for the people of Egypt.

The scribes wrote down the Pharaoh's orders. Their writings tell us about Ancient Egypt.

The priests of Egypt cared for the temples. They held services for the many gods of Ancient Egypt.

The officers of Pharaoh were very important. They carried out the wishes of the Pharaoh.

The Pharaohs of Ancient Egypt were treated like gods. They gave orders to all the people of Egypt.

1   The poorest people in _ _ _ _ _ were the _ _ _ _ _ _ .

2   The farmers of _ _ _ _ _ lived near the _ _ _ _ _ Nile. They grew the
     _ _ _ _ for the people of Egypt.

3   The scribes _ _ _ _ _ down the _ _ _ _ _ _ _ _ ' _ orders. Their
     _ _ _ _ _ _ _ _ _ tell us all about _ _ _ _ _ _ _ Egypt.

4   The _ _ _ _ _ _ _ of Ancient Egypt cared for the _ _ _ _ _ _ _ .

5   The officers of the _ _ _ _ _ _ _ were very important. They _ _ _ _ _ _ _
     out the wishes of the _ _ _ _ _ _ .

6   The Pharaohs of Ancient _ _ _ _ _ were treated like _ _ _ _ .

7   Now carefully draw and colour your own picture of life in Ancient Egypt.

LEVEL

People of Ancient Egypt

The poorest people in Ancient Egypt were the slaves. They had no homes of their own. Their lives were devoted to working for their masters.

The farmers of Ancient Egypt lived close to the River Nile. They grew all the food for the people of Ancient Egypt. They also made things out of wood, stone, reeds, and clay to trade.

The scribes were important people in Ancient Egypt. They wrote the Pharaoh's orders.

The priests of Ancient Egypt were very important people. They looked after the temples and tombs of the Pharaohs. They told the Pharaohs when it was the best time to do certain things, such as go to war.

The officers of the Pharaohs were really important people, they lived in great houses with lots of slaves and scribes to help them. They made sure that the Pharaoh's orders were followed.

The Pharaohs were like gods in Ancient Egypt. They lived in great palaces. They spent a lot of time hunting, playing, feasting and dancing.

A

1 What did the slaves do in Ancient Egypt?

2 Where did the farmers live in Ancient Egypt?

3 Why did the farmers sometimes make things out of wood, stone, clay or reeds?

4 Whose orders did the scribes write out?

5 Why did the officers of the Pharaohs have lots of slaves and scribes to help them?

B

1 Why do you think the priests were very important to the Pharaohs?

2 Why do you think the Pharaohs of Ancient Egypt lived in palaces?

C

Carefully draw and colour your own picture of life in Ancient Egypt.

People of Ancient Egypt

Ancient Egypt had many different groups of people, some more important than others. The least important people in Ancient Egypt were the slaves. They were often people who had been captured by the Egyptians when fighting in distant lands. Slaves had no homes of their own and had to work very hard for their masters.

Next in order in Ancient Egypt came the farmers. They lived with their families close to the River Nile. Many farmers were craftsmen and made articles to trade from wood, stone, clay or papyrus reeds.

Above the farmers in the order of people in Ancient Egypt were the scribes. They were more important because they wrote down all the orders of the Pharaohs, their officers and priests. They also kept the records and accounts for the Pharaohs and their officials. The scribes wrote with ink made from ground up roots, on paper made from papyrus reeds.

The priests of Ancient Egypt came next in the order of people in Ancient Egypt. They were very important because they cared for the temples and tombs for the Pharaohs of Ancient Egypt. They held the services to the different gods the Egyptians worshipped. They foretold the future by studying the moon, the sun and the stars. They would tell the Pharaohs when was the best time to go into battle, or get married or plant the crops.

The second highest rank of people in the order of the people of Ancient Egypt were the officers of the Pharaohs. They were so important that they lived in palaces. They organised all of life in Ancient Egypt. Some were in charge of the army, some in control of the temples and tombs. Others would give the orders to the scribes and farmers about the food supplies for Ancient Egypt, whilst more officers would control the towns and the transport on the River Nile.

At the top of the order of people in Ancient Egypt were the Pharaohs and their families. They were treated like gods by all the other Egyptian peoples. They did not work, they gave orders to their officers, priests and scribes so that all of Egypt was controlled by the Pharaohs. They lived in fine palaces, spent most of their time hunting, fishing, feasting and being entertained. When they died they would be buried in splendid tombs or pyramids.

A

1   Why were the slaves of Ancient Egypt often not Egyptian people?

2   What did the craftsmen farmers of Ancient Egypt make goods from?

3   Where did the farmers of Ancient Egypt live?

4   Why were the scribes of Ancient Egypt more important than the farmers?

5   How did the scribes of Ancient Egypt make their paper and ink?

6   Why did the officers live in palaces in Ancient Egypt?

7   How did the Pharaohs of Ancient Egypt spend most of their time?

B

1   What evidence tells you that the priests could tell the Pharaohs when to go into battle?

2   Why do you think the farmers mainly lived near the River Nile in Ancient Egypt?

3   Why do you think the slaves in Ancient Egypt had no homes of their own?

4   Why do you think that the officers were in charge of different parts of life in Ancient Egypt?

5   What evidence tells you that the Pharaohs were the most important people in Ancient Egypt?

C

Carefully draw and colour your own picture of life in Ancient Egypt.

     LEVEL

People of Ancient Egypt

Ancient Egyptian society was organised rather like a pyramid, at the top of which was the Pharaoh. He was in charge of religion, the law, the army and the government of Egypt. He was treated like a god at times, yet he led a life of great luxury and leisure. He had merely to give an order and other ranks in Ancient Egyptian society would see that it was carried out. The Pharaohs lived in magnificent palaces and indulged in leisure activities such as hunting, fishing, feasting and lavish entertainments.

Below the Pharaohs in the organisation of Ancient Egyptian society came a rank of officers who were in charge of various departments of Egyptian life. The officers may have been in charge of the law, the army, food supplies or control of the Nile waters. Whilst their orders came directly from the Pharaohs, they had immense power throughout Ancient Egyptian life to see that the Pharaoh was obeyed.

Many of the chief officers were relatives of the Pharaohs and lived in fine palaces.

The priests of Ancient Egypt were next in line of rank, for they held important positions as guardian of the temples and tombs of Egypt. The worship of the many royal gods of Egypt was central to the lives of the Pharaohs and they relied on an educated and loyal band of priests to serve their many sites of worship. Again many of the high priests were members of the Royal family and lived a life of luxury, other lower order priests carrying on the daily duties on their behalf. A further task for all priests was to study the sun, moon and stars and forecast the outlook for various events. No Pharaoh embarked on a new course of action without consulting the priests for their predictions as to the outcome of their proposed actions.

Scribes were important because they wrote down all the orders of the Pharaohs, their officers and priests. They also kept the records and accounts for the Pharaohs and their officials. The scribes wrote with ink made from ground up roots, on paper made from papyrus reeds.

Below these upper ranks of Ancient Egyptian life came the farmers and craftsmen. Without this class there would have been insufficient food to make Egypt powerful, and fewer of the magnificent artefacts which have survived to inform historians about Ancient Egyptian society. The farmers held small plots of land from the Pharaoh close to the vital water source of the River Nile. On this fertile land they grew almost all Ancient Egypt's food supplies. To add to their income many made various fine articles in stone, wood, clay, or reeds. These have survived to this day as witness to their skill and artistry.

At the base of the pyramid of Ancient Egyptian society were the slaves who had no homes of their own, little or no wealth and no rights at all. They were owned by richer people and had hard lives dominated by work. Many slaves had been captured in war by the Egyptians and forced into a life of hard work and no pay. The slaves provided the man-power for many of the fine buildings and palaces of Ancient Egypt. Many only lived short lives as death came early due to harsh conditions.

A

1   Why do you think that the Pharaohs had so much leisure time in Ancient Egypt?

2   What do you think the Pharaohs of Ancient Egypt used their army for?

3   What do you think was the main job of the officers of the Pharaohs of Ancient Egypt?

4   What parts of Ancient Egyptian life did the officers of the Pharaoh look after?

5   Why do you think that the officers of Ancient Egypt lived in palaces?

6   Why do you think the priests of Ancient Egypt studied the sun, moon and stars?

7   What evidence tells you that the craftsmen of Ancient Egypt were very skilled?

8   Why do you think the farmers of Ancient Egypt lived close to the River Nile?

B

1   Define the words: society, government, department, organisation.

2   Why do you think the slaves of ancient Egypt lived shorter lives than the Pharaohs?

3   What do you understand by 'educated and loyal band?'

4   Why can historians tell us so much about Ancient Egyptian life?

C

Use reference books to research

(i)   The leisure habits of the Pharaohs of Ancient Egypt.

(ii) The equipment the scribes used for their writing.

Tutankhamun's Tomb

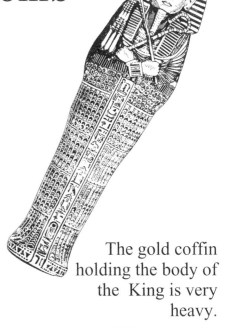

In 1922 in Egypt, Howard Carter found a king's tomb. It had 2,000 rich objects in it.

A jar has a picture of the young king shooting an arrow at deer.

The gold coffin holding the body of the King is very heavy.

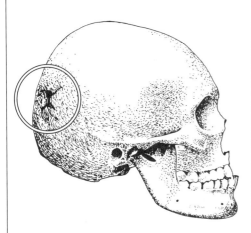

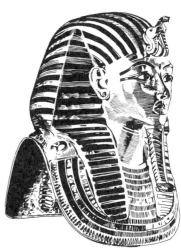

In the King's skull there is a hole. Perhaps he fell from his chariot. He was 18 when he died.

In the tomb there were lots of things for the king to use every day in his after life.

The most famous thing from the King's tomb is a gold mask with jewels. It covers the face of the mummy.

---

1 In 1922, in Egypt, Howard _ _ _ _ _ _ found a _ _ _ _ '_ tomb.

2 A jar has a picture of the _ _ _ _ _ king shooting an _ _ _ _ _ at deer.

3 The gold _ _ _ _ _ _ holding the _ _ _ _ of the king is very heavy.

4 In the King's _ _ _ _ _ there is a hole. Perhaps he fell from his _ _ _ _ _ _ _.

5 In the _ _ _ _ there were lots of things for the King to use _ _ _ _ _ day in his after life.

6 The most _ _ _ _ _ _ thing from the _ _ _ _ '_ tomb is a gold _ _ _ _ .

7 Carefully draw and colour your own picture from the tomb.

       LEVEL

Tutenkhamun's Tomb

In 1922 in the Valley of the Kings in Egypt, Howard Carter, an archaeologist, found the tomb of Pharaoh Tutenkhamun. The tomb had over 2,000 rich treasures in it. He took photos of everything he found in the tomb.

One of the objects, a casket, shows Tutenkhamun throwing a spear at deer and lions from his chariot. Inside the tomb Howard Carter found the coffin of the Pharaoh. It was made of gold and precious gems.

Inside the coffin the skull of the Pharaoh had a hole in it. People think he may have fallen from a chariot or been killed by a spear.

Tutenkhamun was buried with many everyday items like combs, spoons, bows and arrows, and a boat to row, as well as games to play with in his afterlife. A gold mask with jewels was covering the Pharaoh's head.

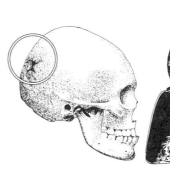

A

1. When was the tomb of Tutenkhamun found?

2. Where was the tomb of Tutenkhamun found?

3. What picture was on the casket found in the Tomb?

4. How do people think that Tutenkhamun died?

5. Which everyday objects were buried in the tomb with Tutenkhamun?

6. Who found the tomb of Tutenkhamun?

B

1. Why do you think that Tutenkhamun was buried with everyday objects?

2. Why was the mask covering the face of the mummy of Tutenkhamun the most amazing item found in the tomb?

C

Carefully draw and colour your own picture from the tomb.

Tutenkhamun's Tomb

In 1922, in the valley of the Kings in Egypt, Howard Carter, an archaeologist, found the Tomb of the Pharaoh Tutenkhamun, which he had been trying to find for over 30 years. The first chamber he opened showed that tomb robbers had been there in ancient times, but once in the inner rooms great treasures were revealed to Carter's eyes. He photographed and wrote careful details of over 2,000 artefacts he found.

Many of these artefacts were every day items such as combs, games, spoons and bows and arrows. These were intended for the dead Tutenkhamun's use in the afterlife.

One of the objects, a beautifully painted casket, has detailed scenes with Tutenkhamun hunting lions and gazelles with his spear from his chariot. Furniture like chairs, tables and chests mean that everything the Pharaoh needed for his comfort were there as well as a boat to cross over into the afterlife.

The most outstanding items were found in the inner-most chamber. First was the amazing gold coffin inset with red, blue and green gemstones, and a wonderful gold and jewelled mask covered the mummys head. These items show how the Pharaohs brought rich goods from the lands that their armies had conquered to make wonderful items for their tombs.

Inside the case was the mummy of Tutenkhamun, his preserved body giving lots of clues as to his life and death. Scientists have found that the body is one of an 18 year old boy. The scientists think that a hole in the skull may have been caused either by a fall from a chariot onto a sharp object or perhaps it came from the thrust of a spear or sword in a murderous attack on the young ruler Tutenkhamun.

A

1   Why did the Pharaohs have every day items with them in their tombs?

2   Where was the tomb of Tutenkhamun found?

3   Why did Carter write down details of all 2,000 items in the tomb?

4   Where were the most precious items in the tomb found?

5   How did Tutenkhamun hunt wild animals?

6   Why was there a boat in the tomb?

7   What do you think caused the death of Tutenkhamun?

B

1   What evidence tells you that the Pharaohs were very rich?

2   Why do you think Carter photographed every item he found in the tomb?

3   Why do you think it was called the Valley of the Kings?

4   Why do you think there were items of furniture in the tomb?

5   What evidence tells you where the gold and precious gem stones came from?

C

Carefully draw and colour your own picture from the tomb.

 LEVEL

Tutenkhamun's Tomb

Howard Carter was an archaeologist who was interested in Ancient Egypt. He had been searching for the hidden tomb of the Egyptian Pharaoh Tutenkhamun in the valley of the Kings in Egypt for 30 years. In 1922 he found the entrance to a tomb. When he broke in he found that the tomb was almost intact. Grave robbers way back in time had only disturbed the outer chamber.

When Carter opened up the inner chambers, he was amazed by the great wealth of artefacts buried with the young Pharaoh. There were over 2,000 precious items revealing vast amounts of information about life and death in 1323 B.C. Carter's first task was to photograph every single item and then record as much detail as possible about each object for future students.

The chambers of the tomb were crammed with artefacts, which had been selected to help the dead Pharaoh in his journey into the afterlife. There were everyday things like combs, brushes, games and hunting spears.

But it was the gold coffin case, inset with rich stones of blue, green and red, which astonished Carter and his workers when they entered the inner-most chamber. Even grander was a mask fitting over the head of the mummy that was Tutenkhamun. Its splendour shows how rich the Egyptian Pharaohs were, and how much they relied on the rich objects and raw materials plundered from countries far away from their borders that their armies had conquered.

Amongst the funeral goods were many items of richly decorated furniture. One casket had a delicately painted hunting scene around its edges. Tutenkhamun was portrayed hurling hunting spears at fleeing lions and gazelles during a royal hunting expedition on the fringes of the desert.

When the mummified body was examined it revealed the skeleton of an 18 year old, who by his chest contents seemed to have been suffering from tuberculosis. A hole in the skull suggested to scientists a violent blow either from a fall from a horse or perhaps a murderous death at the point of a spear. The Tomb of Tutenkhamun is one of the great treasures of world history yet a site of great mystery.

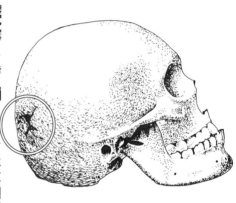

A

1 Why did Howard Carter find the outer chamber of Tutenkhamun's tomb disturbed?

2 What do you think kept Howard Carter searching for Tutenkhamun's tomb for 30 years?

3 Why do you think the artefacts buried with Tutenkhamun's mummy give historians ideas about Ancient Egyptian life?

4 What date was Tutenkhamun born?

5 Why do you think the Pharaoh Tutenkhamun needed hunting spears buried with him?

6 Why do you think Tutenkhamun's coffin was made of gold and rich stones?

7 How do scientists think Tutenkhamun might have been murdered?

8 Why did Howard Carter photograph each item from the tomb?

B

1 Define the words:
Archaeologist, artefacts, mummified

2 What do you think was the reason for Carter recording all the detail of each item found in the Tomb?

3 What do you understand by 'funeral goods'?

4 What caused the Egyptian Pharaohs to have such riches in their tombs?

C

Use reference books to research:

(i) The process of preserving bodies as Mummies

(ii) The Egyptians beliefs about the afterlife.

Time to Spare Activities

1 Write the diary of a scribe at Tutenkhamun's palace for 2 days.

2 Make a model of one of the Ancient Egyptian gods.

3 Make an Egyptian bedroom in a shoe box.

4 Write a letter from a Pharaoh to the builder of his pyramids.

5 Design and make an Egyptian hunting chariot.

6 Research all you can about papyrus used for writing by the Ancient Egyptians.

7 Draw a picture of Ancient Egyptians getting water from the Nile.

8 Write the diary of an Ancient Egyptian Pharaoh for 3 days.

9 Design your own Ancient Egyptian costume for a special feast.

10 Find out why the kings of Ancient Egypt were called Pharaohs.

11 Draw the weapons Ancient Egyptian soldiers used.

12 Write a sentence in Ancient Egyptian Hieroglyphics.

13 Research all you can about Cleopatra.

14 Design your own Ancient Egyptian temple.

15 Make a poster of land transport in Ancient Egypt.

16 Research all you can about the meaning of Ancient Egyptian town names.

17 Make a wall map of Ancient Egypt.

18 List the equipment in an Ancient Egyptian kitchen and compare it with a modern kitchen.

19 Write an account of the building of an Ancient Egyptian house.

20 Make a poster advertising a feast day in an Ancient Egyptian palace.

21 Make your own design book of Egyptian pottery.

22 Research as much as you can about Ancient Egyptian children's games.

23 Design your own Ancient Egyptian necklace.

24 Make your own booklet about Ancient Egyptian musical instruments.

25 Make a poster of Ancient Egyptian boats.

26 Make your own model of an Ancient Egyptian mask.

26 Make your own Ancient Egyptian wall mural showing people fishing in the Nile.

27 Make a catalogue of Ancient Egyptian tools.

28 Make your own booklet about soldiers in Ancient Egypt.

30 Make a catalogue of the animals of Ancient Egypt.

31 Design your own Egyptian palace.

32 Make your own catalogue of fashions in dress for Ancient Egypt.

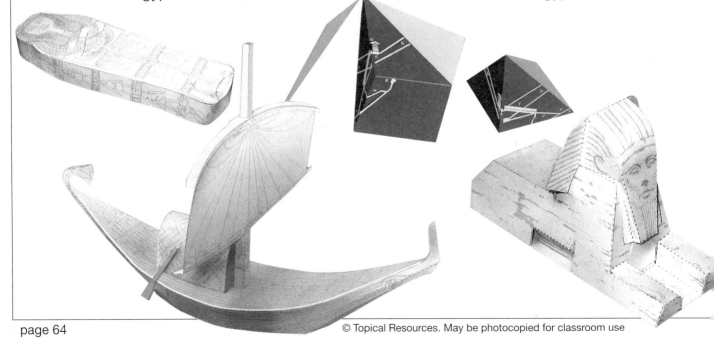